Activities with Senior Adults

ROGER L. HAUSER is minister to senior adults, Calvary Baptist Church, Savannah, Georgia. He was formerly a senior adult consultant, Family Ministry Department, Sunday School Board of the Southern Baptist Convention, Nashville, Tennessee. He is a husband and father.

Activities with SENIOR ADULTS

Roger L. Hauser

BROADMAN PRESS
Nashville, Tennessee

1987

© Copyright 1987 ● Broadman Press
All rights reserved
4239-01

ISBN: 0-8054-3901-3

Dewey Decimal Classification: 259.3
Subject Heading: CHURCH WORK WITH THE ELDERLY

Library of Congress Catalog Card Number: 87-13898
Printed in the United States of America

Library of Congress Cataloging-in-Publication Data

Hauser, Roger L., 1951-
    Activities with senior adults.

    Bibliography: p. 145
    1. Church work with the aged. 2. Church work with
the aged—Southern Baptist Convention.   3. Southern
Baptist Convention.   4. Baptists—United States.
I. Title.
BV4435.H38 1987   259'.3   87-13898
ISBN 0-8054-3901-3

Dedication

This resource book is lovingly dedicated to my wife, Donna, and to our two children, Lauren and David. They have been supportive and nurturing and have enriched my life to the point of encouraging me to write this book. I love you.

Preface

Welcome to a book of new and fresh programming ideas for senior adult ministry.

This book was written to give pastors, church staff members with senior adult responsibility, ministers of senior adults, club program presidents, and volunteer lay leaders ideas for creative ministry.

It is important to note that every senior adult program is unique in needs and interests. Each church would be wise to conduct a needs and interest survey to determine special concerns. Horace Kerr's book *How to Minister to Senior Adults in Your Church* (Nashville: Broadman Press, 1980) gives explicit instructions on conducting a valid survey.

This book is unique due to the design of special programming for churches. This section deals with important issues and national needs of older persons. Other divisions include a biblical rationale for ministry with the aging, a brief historical overview of Southern Baptist work with senior adults, creative ministry ideas which have been successful, and club programming suggestions. I believe the "Resources" section to be a most important one; one of the greatest needs of senior adult leadership is how to find and access national, private, and religious resources for activities.

As you begin reading the book, help yourself to being creative in ministry, which has at its primary root not the human mind, but the creative potential and desire for excellence in God alone.

ROGER L. HAUSER

Contents

Man's mind, once stretched by a new idea,
never regains its original dimensions.

OLIVER WENDELL HOLMES

1
A Rationale
for Senior Adult Ministry

A Rationale for Senior Adult Ministry

Why do we have senior adult ministry in our local churches? What should be the perimeters of such an organization? How should it be administered? These questions and more are answered in detail in Horace Kerr's book *How to Minister to Senior Adults in Your Church*. Horace Kerr is the supervisor of the senior adult section of the Family Ministry Department at the Baptist Sunday School Board. His book is considered to be a model for helping churches to develop and expand their aging ministries.

This resource manual expands Kerr's book by tying into the basic organization he has outlined with suggested component ministries in his proposed five needs and interests areas: spiritual enrichment, socialization, learning opportunities, service opportunities, and services needed. Each component or activity suggestion will show how it ties into the overall program, a description and need for the component, and resources for further study.

It is to be assumed that any component activity implemented in a church is done so as a result of a needs-and-interest survey conducted prior to the activity being promoted. We must remember that a senior adult ministry is by, for, and with senior adults.

15

It is their ministry, and they should be allowed to develop their own programming.

The bottom line of why have a senior adult ministry is that the church is endeavoring to bring older adults from a lower aim of living to a higher aim. Gerontologists have one common goal: to determine ways to enhance the quality of life in the later years. The message of Christ speaks directly to that issue for all humanity.

Vern Bengston of the Andrus Gerontology Center in California has said that "the central questions of the field are much what they were two decades ago, how can we add years to life? How can we add life to years? We're more concerned with the second question."

The basic rationale for developing ministries with senior adults is to provide meaningful activities in a person's retirement years that will add *quality* to a person's life. We remember the words of Jesus when He said, "I am come that they might have life, and that they might have it more abundantly" (John 10:10).

A proper rationale for aging ministries has at its root the biblical statement. Throughout the scriptural record there are many statements pertaining to the older person.

Older persons are not to be pitied or ignored but challenged and utilized for greater service to their Lord and church. Seniors are persons of worth whom God created.

ABRAHAM MASLOW'S HIERARCHY OF NEEDS

H
i
g
h
e
r

Need for

SELF-ACTUALIZATION

To develop to one's fullest capacity as a human being; to find meaning
in life; to find answers to life's questions.

O
r
d
e
r

ESTEEM NEEDS

Sense of adequacy, of competence, of achievement, of contribution;
recognition, prestige.

BELONGINGNESS AND LOVE NEEDS

The need for affection, inclusion, place in one's group.

L
o
w
e
r

SAFETY NEEDS

Security, protection against physical threats; familiarity and stability of
the environment.

O
r
d
e
r

PHYSIOLOGICAL NEEDS

For food, housing, clothing, health care, mobility.

The fruit of the biblical foundation is the quality component ministries and activities that the church offers through the church.

All component activities should reflect the needs and interests of the local congregation. Every idea in this book will not work in every church—only if that need has been expressed.

In the chart on page 17 you will see the hierarchy of needs that Abraham Maslow developed. This hierarchy can be applied to our seniors. What are we doing to enable our older persons to reach "self-actualization" in their lives? How are we strengthening their "esteem needs," "belongingness and love needs," "safety needs," and "physiological needs"?

According to a study conducted by the Gerontology Center at Duke University, the top six major concerns of a national survey of retirees listed: adequate income, unemployment, health, where to live, loneliness, and lack of aim. What is the church doing to meet the physical, social, and emotional needs of our senior adults?

According to the Independent News Alliance, President Ronald Reagan wants American churches to help the needy and make up for federal budget cuts. Reagan has given seniors thought to challenging the churches. En route to a "private sector" speech one fall day, the president looked out the car window and said, "If the churches would just respond to community needs . . . ."

By designing ministries through our churches, we

can reach our retirees as well as touch the lives of those in our communities. Our philosophy of aging ministry should be community-wide.

Let's determine to "tap the resources" of our senior adults, utilizing their talents, skills, and abilities to provide *quality* programming in the days and years ahead.

Again, the components will be based on the five needs-and-interests areas of Kerr's book.

1. Spiritual Enrichment
2. Socialization
3. Learning Opportunities
4. Service Opportunities
5. Services Needed

The basic process of implementing this ministry is further explained in Kerr's book, but the following is a skeletal outline of the process:

1. Church votes to call a senior adult coordinator.
2. Form Task Force.
3. Give orientation for Task Force on survey.
4. Task Force surveys community resources and programs.
5. Elect church survey captains.
6. Compile a list of all senior adults in church.
7. Conduct the survey one on one.
8. Tabulate results.
9. Decide on direction.
10. Evaluate.

The component ministries on pages 27-30 were developed at Calvary Baptist Temple in Savannah,

Georgia, over a period of two years with over 150 different persons serving on 31 committees. The success of the program at Calvary is that the activities and ministries evolved out of a survey of over 1,100 senior adults. The programming was by, for, and with the senior adults. It was their program.

All programs may not be as large in scope, but they can be just as effective and meaningful in a smaller church environment. Include relevant telephone numbers for information and reservations.

The primary reason for a ministry with senior adults lies in a fundamental teaching of the Bible, the worth of the person. Jesus said, "I am come that they might have life, and that they might have it more abundantly" (John 10:10). This abundant living is for all of life. The individual may expect it; the church is the instrument of God to assure one's having it.

By the year 2000, the average American will have twenty years of life remaining after retirement. In 1900 the average life expectancy was forty-seven years, and only one person in twenty-five was over sixty-five years of age. In 1980, one in every eight to ten persons was sixty-five and above, and the 28 million older Americans of 1980 will increase to over 32 million by the year 2000. According to the US Bureau of the Census, the number of people over sixty-five years of age will increase in the next ten years by 4.1 million or 22 percent.

In most Southern Baptist churches, senior adults comprise about 20 percent of the memberships. The gap between this group and other church members needs to be closed; but if this is to be done, the elderly must be known as individuals, not as stereotypes. We need to understand the problems of our senior adults and endeavor to see them in the broadest sense possible. Until the problems are seen in their true perspective, the way in which a church approaches a ministry with senior adults will not be effective.

Basic to our approach is the need to understand a Christian theology of ministry with senior adults. Throughout the Bible are humanitarian doctrines that provide a framework for action pertinent to the aging. The supreme worth of every human being, created in the image of God, is one of the basic teachings of the Bible. "God saw every thing that he had made, and, behold, it was very good" (Gen. 1:31). Christians believe in God as the Creator and Redeemer of life, as well as that they themselves are the creations of God's love. These two basic convictions encompass the spiritual needs of older adults: assurance of God's love, a sense of meaning and purpose, a desire for security, freedom from the loneliness of life, a sense of being wanted, and the love and understanding of other people.

Who are senior adults, the ones whom we wish to program for? They are God's creations. The first man was apparently created an adult, but humans are in the image of God throughout their entire lives. The older, wrinkled face topped by gray or sparse hair and supported by a weakened body is no less the image of God than the younger, stronger figure. Theologically, being a creation of God gives every Christian worth throughout life.

As we study what the Bible has to say regarding senior adults, we find many references which emphasize the importance of this group. The Old Testament declares that longevity is a special blessing of God—"If thou wilt walk in my ways, to keep my statutes and my commandments, as thy father David did walk, then I will lengthen thy days" (1 Kings 3:14)—and states that older persons are deserving of honor, respect, and recognition: "Thou shalt rise up before the hoary head, and honour the face of the old man, and fear thy God: I am the Lord" (Lev. 19:32). Wisdom and maturity also generally accompany old age: "With the ancient is wisdom; and in the length of days understanding" (Job 12:12). The Bible also says old age is a normal part of life: "To every thing there is a season, and a time to every purpose under the heaven: A time to be born, and a time to die" (Eccl. 3:1-2*a*).

Another passage of Scripture which will be discussed in more detail here is Isaiah 46:4:

> Even to your old age I am He,
>   and to gray hairs I will carry you.
> I have made, and I will bear;
>   I will carry and will save (RSV).

The latter years of one's life are a time of fulfillment of promises and the receiving of rewards. In the New Testament emphasis on respect for the older person continues: "Rebuke not an elder, but entreat him as a father; and the younger men as brethren; The elder women as mothers; the younger as sisters, with all purity" (1 Tim. 5:1-2). Older persons are to set an example for and instruct the younger. This could provide impetus for the development of an educational program in the church staffed by older adults, utilizing their talents and skills to teach others. Reference is also made to care being provided for widows: "Pure religion and undefiled before God and the Father is this, To visit the fatherless and widows in their affliction" (Jas. 1:27).

The Bible has much to say concerning the older person. Therefore, the church has an obligation to aid this quasi-minority group. The church is to assist them in achieving their fullest potential as individuals responsible to God and to their society. In the context of this obligation, neglecting senior adults in our church programming would be unthinkable for two reasons. First, even though an individual may have lived a long life, no one ever reaches a state of perfection; second, senior adults can continue to grow and have a fulfilled life through the proper programming of a local church.

Three basic passages of Scripture reveal the worth of the older person in the eyes of God. The first passage (Job 12:12) shows the older person's worth as a possessor of wisdom and knowledge. The second (Isa. 46:4) will be examined here to show the worth of the elderly individual in the fact that God will never leave him or her but will constantly support these individuals in their daily needs. The last scriptural exegesis will show God's concern for the widows' worth (Jas. 1:27) in the admonition that the church should take the responsibility of caring for them.

"With the ancient is wisdom; and in length of days understanding" (Job 12:12). The word *ancient* means an old man, graybearded. It is used chiefly in poetry and connotes the sense of one who is decrepit with age. The meaning of the passage is that wisdom may be expected to be found in the one who has a long opportunity to observe the course of events, who has conversed with a former generation, and who has time for personal reflection. This sentiment is in accordance with ancient Oriental views in which knowledge was imparted primarily by tradition, and wisdom depended much on the opportunity for personal observation. The connection of thought is that humans acquire knowledge by the senses—the eye that sees, the ear that hears, the palate that tastes— and they attain wisdom by long experience.

The next passage of Scripture is Isaiah 46:4: "Even to your old age I am he; and even to hoar hairs will I carry you: I have made, and I will bear; even I will carry, and will deliver you." According to *The Broadman Bible Commentary,* in this verse people "are told that he who made them in the beginning will bear them to old age and will save them." God is revealing to the older person that he has worth and dignity to the extent that He says, "I am the same." "I do not change," God declares throughout the Scriptures; He has the same tenderness, the same affection, and the same concern for the older individual as He does for anyone else.

Here the care of God for His people surpasses that of the most tender parent. The care of the parent naturally diminishes as a child reaches adulthood, and the parent oftentimes is removed by death before the son or daughter who elicited so much care in infancy and childhood reaches old age. But this is not so with God. His people always need His care and are always the objects of His tender mercy. Age does not make them less dependent, and experience only teaches them more of their need for His direction and His grace.

The doctrine is that God's people always need His protection and care, that He who is the God of infancy and childhood will be the God of the aged, and that He will not leave or forsake His people, who have been the objects of His care and affection in childhood, when they become old. By using one's imagination, one can almost hear the prophet singing to his people, "Be not dismayed whate'er betide, God will take care of you."

That the elderly have the same worth before God as they had in their youth is of utmost importance in the doctrine of God. Once our churches understand that, they will program as energetically for older adults as they do for younger people. James 1:27 states, "Pure religion and undefiled before God and the Father is this, To visit the fatherless and widows in their affliction." In Old Testament times, widows were specially cared for and protected by God. It is not surprising, therefore, that in New Testament times we would find widows cared for with even deeper tenderness.

Any rationale for ministry with senior adults must have a theological basis. Through this discussion of passages from Scripture we have seen the need for ministry as well as biblical admonitions to minister to, with, and through older church members. All ministries must speak to the uniqueness of the individual and the church. Theologically, all our programming, activities, and ministries must strive to increase the quality of life of our senior adults. To God be the glory for what He can do through the senior saints of our churches.

THE
CALVARY
BAPTIST
TEMPLE

**Baptist
Senior Adults**

Psalm 1:3

Senior
Adult
Ministry

Fall Semester Program

Jesus
"I am come that they might have life, and that they might have it more abundantly."

John 10:10

—*"THE CHURCH THAT CARES—*

(page one)

SENIOR ADULT MINISTRY

ACTIVITY COMPONENTS

━━━━━━━━━━ **SPIRITUAL ENRICHMENT** ━━━━━━━

1. **Sunday School**—9:30 AM Sundays (Three Senior Adult Departments with 18 classes)
2. **Outreach Bible Classes**—Jack Reid (Bible teaching in 7 nursing homes)
3. **Extension Ministry**—Mildred Gooding (Shut-in visitation)
4. **Weekday Bible Study Class**—Don Venn (Wednesdays, 10:00 A.M.)

━━━━━━━━━ **LEARNING OPPORTUNITIES** ━━━━━━

1. **Church Training**— 5:45 PM Sundays
2. **Senior Adult Resource Center** (Library for senior adults)
3. **Senior Center for Continuing Education** (Schedule on back)
4. **"Aging: The New Frontier"**
5. **Monthly Newsletter**

━━━━━━━━━ **SERVICE OPPORTUNITIES** ━━━━━━

1. **Music Ministry**—Rick Forbus
2. **Woman's Missionary Union**—Jewell Banks
3. **Volunteer Service Corps**—Linday Dyches (Ministry opportunities for older adults)
4. **"Citadels"**—Rick Forbus (Senior adult choir, Wednesdays, 12:30 PM)
5. **Senior Adult Evangelism**—Roger Hauser (Wednesdays, 11:45 AM)
6. **Dixie Ragtime Minstrels,** Phyllis Goethe, Porter Dawson

(page two)

1. **"Diamond Set"**—Lukie Bass, President
   (General meeting of senior adults on last Tuesday of each month.)
2. **Trip and Travel**—Margaret Barbee
   (Monthly trips—separate brochure for 1984)
3. **Ceramics**—Alva Selbo
   (Tuesdays, 10:00 AM)
4. **Exercise Class**—John Yandle, Jean Schexnayder
   (Wednesdays, 11:00 AM)
5. **Bowling League**—Wadie Moreland
   (Friday, 10:00 AM)

━━━━━━━━━━ SERVICES NEEDED ━━━━━━━━━

1. **Telephone Reassurance**—Elsie Tryan
   (Daily telephone call for shut-in)
2. **Social Service Consultant**—Florrie Moore.
   Call church for appointment.
3. **Legal Advice Consultant**—Ray Gaskin
   Call church for appointment.
4. **Job Bank**—Linda Dyches
   (To help secure employment for senior adults)
5. **"Futrell's Diner"** Lunch daily at 12:00 noon at church. Call church the day before for reservations. (Cost $1.50)
6. **Transportation**—Faye Dyches
7. **Convalescent Supplies**—Marguerite Anderson, (wheelchairs, walkers, etc.)
8. **Handyman Services,** Charles Crews
9. **Adopt-A-Grandparent,** Jack Reid
10. **Personal Service** (haircut and set), Barbara Shuman

"AGING: THE NEW FRONTIER"
8:00 PM Alternate Thursdays
Cable Channel 7

This Calvary-produced program will focus on issues affecting the older person - issues such as social security, community resources, retirement, and many more informative subjects.

If you have suggestions for future programming, please contact Roger Hauser at:

Calvary Baptist Temple
4625 Waters Avenue
Savannah, GA 31404

(page three)

CALVARY SENIOR CENTER
FOR CONTINUING EDUCATION
Activities Building
Monday - Friday

MONDAYS
12:00 PM   Lunch ("Futrell's Diner")

TUESDAYS
10:00 AM   Ceramics
11:00 AM   "Diamond Set" (last Tuesday)
12:00 PM   Lunch

WEDNESDAYS
9:30 AM   Coffee and Doughnuts
10:00 AM   Weekday Bible Class
11:00 AM   Exercise Class
11:45 AM   Evangelism Training
12:00 PM   Lunch
12:30 PM   "Citadels" (Choir Room)

THURSDAYS
11:00 AM   Dixie Ragtime Minstrels (Fourth Thursdays)
12:00 PM   Lunch

FRIDAYS
10:00 AM   Bowling League, Major League Lanes
12:00 PM   Lunch

INFORMATION AND REFERRAL:

Roger Hauser, Minister of Senior Adults

Linda Dyches, Sr. Ad. Special Ministries Coordinator

Phyllis Goethe, Special Assistant
Jack Reid, Church Visitor

Joyce Humphrey, Youth and Senior Adult Secretary

CALVARY BAPTIST TEMPLE
4625 Waters Avenue
Savannah, GA 31404

(page four)

2
A Brief History
of Southern Baptist Work
with Senior Adults

A Brief History of Southern Baptist Work with Senior Adults

Concern for the aging population has always existed in the religious community. Even during the early years of Judeo-Christian growth, the older person was a vital part of community life. Early Christians paid marks of respect to the elderly and ascribed to them a significant spiritual role. Ministry with the elderly involves caring for each individual as a person created in the image of God and, thus, a person of worth. Traditionally, old age within the religious community is considered the positive and good fulfillment of a life devoted to God.

The elderly of the early church comprised a smaller percentage of its members than in the church today; due to the advances of modern medicine and hygiene, more people reach older adulthood and experience the needs and problems that often develop during the later years. Within the world of Judeo-Christian aging ministry, a number of programs have been initiated to aid this quasi-minority group of the elderly. This chapter presents a small part of what is being done within the religious community at large.

For a historical overview, one must survey the history of aging ministry in the Southern Baptist Convention. Since 1953 the Convention has been verbally and actively interested in varied forms of ministry with the elderly. In a *Watchman Examiner* article S. L. Morgan stated, "Society and churches are just beginning to rub their eyes and see the problem (of aging) in its appalling bigness and acuteness. . . . In the average church and community, the aged and shut-ins are pitiably neglected." In 1954 John Carter—also in the *Watchman Examiner*—wrote, "In recent years, strong emphasis has been made on the ministry to youth and rightly so; but has there not been a tendency at times to build a church around young people to the practical exclusion of older folks and the service they can render?"

Morgan and Carter were instrumental in provoking Southern Baptists to do some serious thinking in regard to an organized effort to promote ministry and component activities with the aging in the Convention and within local churches. In 1956 the Christian Life Commission, an agency within the Southern Baptist Convention dealing with social and ethical issues, called the first Southern Baptist Conference on Aging. This conference helped to further the awareness of aging ministry within the church. Local churches and agencies within various state Baptist conventions began to expand their aging ministries due to the exposure created by this conference.

In 1960 the first aging ministry course taught at an accredited seminary was presented by James D. Williams, professor of adult education at Southwestern Baptist Theological Seminary in Fort Worth, Texas.

Southern, Golden Gate, and Midwestern Baptist Theological Seminaries of the Southern Baptist Convention now also have courses dealing with the aging ministry, and the New Orleans and Southeastern Baptist Seminaries offer several varied courses which include aging content. Of fifty-four Southern Baptist colleges, approximately one half offer undergraduate courses in gerontology, usually in the department of sociology.

Southwestern Baptist Theological Seminary presently offers a joint degree program in studies in aging in conjunction with the Center for Studies in Aging at North Texas State University in Denton, Texas. The seminary has additional plans to develop an interdisciplinary program which would include aging courses in several departments such as social work, recreation, preaching, and music. The seminary's continuing education program plans workshops in aging.

The Executive Committee of Homes for the Aging of the Southern Baptist Convention was formed in 1963. In 1972 its name was changed to the Southern Baptist Association of Ministries with the Aging (SBAMA), and its functions were enlarged to include all levels of work with the aging. In 1981 the association voted to allow state conventions and educational institutions to establish chapters. The first chapter was organized in that year at Southwestern Baptist Theological Seminary. Members of the chapter have interests in aging ministry, and it is open to both students and faculty. Other chapters are active in Texas and Georgia.

In 1973 the Southern Baptist Convention in its annual meeting adopted a resolution calling for a study of the aging. Gary Cook, a graduate of the Center for Studies in Aging at North Texas State University and of The Southern Baptist Theological Seminary, called for this resolution. A conference on aging was held in Nashville, Tennessee, in October 1974 as a part of that study. The conference closed with a verbal recognition of the need of senior adults (the term *senior adults* means those individuals within the Southern Baptist Convention aged sixty and above). The recommendations cited the need for a group who will serve as "special advocates on the part of aging members."

As a result of this declaration, a Southern Baptist Convention Advisory Group on aging was established with representatives from the Sunday School Board, Home Mission Board, Annuity Board, Foreign Mission Board, seminaries, Christian Life Commission, Brotherhood Commission, Woman's Missionary Union, and co-opted members from state conventions, Baptist colleges, and various other Southern Baptist agencies and committees. The Advisory Group is associated with the Church Program Subcommittee of the Coordinating Committee of the Inter-Agency Council.

In 1975 leaders at the Baptist Sunday School Board decided that, in addition to the interest and efforts being put forth by aging programs, a valid need existed for a specialized section responsible for developing and promoting models of programming and ministry with and for the aging. Consequently, the senior adult section of the Family Ministry Department was organized. The senior adult section has five objectives in its assigned task from the Sunday School Board.

1. Create in Baptist leadership and members an awareness of the worth and needs of senior adults.

2. Promote among denominational workers, pastors, other church members an awareness of the worth and needs of senior adults, and among members of all ages a better understanding of the aging process and life in the later years.

3. Assist state conventions, associations, and churches to meet the needs of senior adults, particularly in the areas of spiritual growth, social interaction, meaningful service opportunities, continuing education, and special services.

4. Provide means by which senior adult Baptists throughout the nation can engage in fellowship with each other.

Cooperate with all departments of the Sunday School Board and other Baptist agencies in providing a comprehensive system of programming for and with senior adults.

The strategies for accomplishing these objectives include publications, national conferences, church plans, and field services. The publications of the senior adult section are *Mature Living,* a magazine with over 300,000 subscribers; a developmental-needs book per year; a family enrichment series; and a National Association of Baptist Senior Adult news-letter, *The Gazette.* This organization presently has over 32,000 members.

Various national conferences include the annual Senior Adult Chautauquas, ten weeks of conferences for senior adults and training for leadership. Semi-nars are conducted at the Church Program Training Center in Nashville and in five Southern Baptist seminaries.

Program designs for various churches include lead-ership training workshops, seminars, and confer-ences. Horace Kerr, supervisor of the Senior Adult Ministry Section, authored *How to Minister to Senior Adults in Your Church* in 1980 to provide a model to churches in designing aging ministries. The senior adult section has also designated the first Sunday in May as Senior Adult Day on the Convention calen-dar. A brochure is written annually for churches to plan Senior Adult Day.

Within the "young" history of Southern Baptist ministry with the aging, the senior adult section of the Sunday School Board will prove to be the catalyst for an expanded Senior Adult Ministry within the local church and various state conventions. The "seed" that was planted by Morgan and Carter in the early 1950s is now coming to fruition. Since the 1974 Southern Baptist Conference on Aging, much has been accomplished in regard to awareness and programming of aging ministries.

Seven years after the Conference, James D. Williams responded in a personal interview to its recommended actions. These actions were proposed by Williams and are contained in a pamphlet entitled *Where Do We Go from Here?* and based upon his closing address. Williams, who is now executive vice-president of the Baptist Sunday School Board, has provided leadership and guidance in the area of Senior Adult Ministry within the Southern Baptist Convention.

The first recommended action mentioned was made with regard to communication. Higher visibility from all agencies and boards is needed in addition to expanded content of materials written and filmed for leadership as well as for older persons themselves.

The second suggestion indicated that the primary responsibility for the implementation of this ministry rests with the local church. The needs of older adults, Williams stated, can best be met at a local level. Therefore, churches must have (1) trained leaders who understand the elderly and their needs, (2) materials that point up the biblical responsibility of churches to minister to those needs, (3) strategies of evangelism that reflect the special needs of older persons, (4) flexible and practical suggestions on how to organize and implement ministries, and (5) encouragement in establishing cooperative commitments with ongoing community services that are already at work on behalf of older persons.

A third action proposed is in the area of advocacy. Southern Baptists need to be challenged to advocacy at the point of critical issues of discrimination and stereotyping.

The fourth action proposed by Williams is training future leaders in aging ministry through seminaries and schools. Too few Southern Baptist ministers are trained to understand that the older adult is struggling with life-and-death problems.

The final action recommended in *Where Do We Go from Here?* is increased intergenerational dialogue and study, specifying that committees and boards have a balanced number of older and younger persons.

The goal of this book is to assist local church leaders to develop progressive senior adult programs with resources provided to aid further study and to continue to expand the horizons of an aging ministry across the Convention.

3
The Minister of Senior Adults

The Minister of Senior Adults

Qualifications

The minister of senior adults should be an individual with an intrinsic motivation to minister with older persons. Education in the field of gerontology or training in senior adult ministry would be essential for a person ministering in this capacity. One must have an understanding of the unique and varied needs of older adults to be able to effectively minister with them.

The minister of senior adults can be an individual of any age or sex. The important point is that he or she be able to relate. He must be loving, warm, and sincere. Older persons respond positively to sincerity and friendliness.

The motivation of the minister of senior adults is important. A leader of senior adults who is motivated by a need for attention will not be effective in developing independence and in fostering programs developed by the senior adults themselves.

This person must recognize older persons as persons of worth. He must work *with* the older adults, not to or for them. He should strive to enrich their lives through the basic programs of the church and those which they themselves develop and operate.

The minister of senior adults must not be a negative, patronizing, dogmatic, or highly emotional person. She must realize that she does not have all the answers. She is there to be a learner as well as a leader.

The leader should know how to handle overexpressions of appreciation that he will be receiving. He should be careful to avoid the spotlight and to make a sincere effort to shift responsibility and praise to the older persons themselves.

Management, public relations, promotion, and advocacy skills are highly desirable in the ministry of senior adults.

Responsibilities

The responsibilities of the minister of senior adults fall into two categories: general and specific. The general responsibilities of the senior adult minister would be to serve as the primary staff resource person for senior adult ministries, assuming specific leadership roles as opportunities and needs afford.

The minister of senior adults should also develop and work with appropriate organizational structures to build, maintain, and expand through a comprehensive and coordinated ministry so that if this position were vacant, the ministry would continue.

Specific responsibilities would include the following:

1. Create an awareness of the worth and needs of senior adults.

2. Promote a better understanding of the aging process and life in the later years.
3. Build and continue a program of ministry which meets the specific needs of older persons around these contest areas: socialization, spiritual, learning opportunities, service opportunities, and services needed.
4. Coordinate the activities of the church base programs and emphases which relate to older persons.
5. Implement special ministries according to specific needs for and with nursing homes and homebound senior adults.
6. Serve as a liaison with other congregations' senior adult ministries, denominational programs, and community programs and agencies which seek to meet the needs of older persons.
7. Work closely with pastor regarding pastoral and senior adult ministries.
8. Serve as chairperson of the senior adult task force to determine needs and interests of senior adults and establish the direction of the senior adult program.
9. Serve as chairperson of the senior adult council formed after the task force has completed its work.
10. Work closely with the senior adult club officers in planning and conducting the club programs.
11. Act as liaison between all church programs serving senior adults.

12. Maintain relationships with community organizations serving the elderly.
13. Correlate and coordinate all activities of senior adults in the church through an annual calendar of activities developed through the senior adult council.
14. Report all senior adult activities to the church through regular church procedures.
15. Publish a monthly newsletter for all senior adults of the church.
16. Recommend actions for the church to take to enhance the senior adult ministry, such as building improvements, budgeting for special needs, special services to those in need, and church-wide features such as the annual Senior Adult Day (first Sunday in May).
17. Produce, through the television ministry, a program targeted at the older adult population of the church and city.

Guidelines

The minister of senior adults should organize her workday so as to be available in the church office at a specified time and to work at least five days a week.

He is expected to attend staff meetings, all general meetings of the church, and, when possible, committees and groups within the church.

She is expected to keep informed as to the best in education and administration by engaging in personal study, attending clinics, conferences, and assemblies.

He should serve in associational and denominational work as time permits.

Relationships

The minister of senior adults is to cooperate totally and confidentially with the congregation, organizational leadership, pastor and staff in regards to the total church program.

The minister of senior adults is directly responsible to the pastor and the minister of education-administration with associate responsibilities and relationships to other staff members in their particular area of specialization.

Etiquette

The minister's behavior should be based on the behavior and etiquette that is observed in the teachings of Jesus Christ.

The minister of senior adults should be completely natural, entirely himself, treating older persons with a natural friendliness. He should respect each person, never condescending in tone, word, or manner. He should speak clearly, repeating instructions when needed, and patiently take time to experiment with an activity until all understand what to do. He should take responsibility for bringing new ideas and suggestions to the group.

Above all, she should never judge people hastily

but seek out the cause of aggressiveness or other objectionable characteristics. She should never talk disparagingly about one person to another.

Conclusion

A senior adult ministry is an effort to channel and utilize the talents and energy of this group at this strategic time in their lives. The genius of a senior adult ministry is that it speaks to, utilizes the talents of, and, therefore, specifically reaches the senior adults in the church and community.

4
Issues Programming

Issue: Ministry Target Group

When we explore senior adult ministry, we are primarily looking at the retired individual. Why?

"Retirement Can Be Hazardous," an article by Joe Purvis in the Savannah *Morning News*, stated: "The average male retires and dies between 30 and 40 months afterward. Alcoholism and mental illness plague a disproportionate number of retirees. Men over 65 account for a quarter of the suicides in the United States."

He also stated that "according to a study by the National Institute of Mental Health, a third of all marriages decline after retirement." He concluded by saying, "Retirement, per se, is looked upon by the American Medical Association as a health hazard."

Retirement years can be fulfilling, but to many, life is only an existence. Our philosophy should say "re-tread," not "retire."

An effective senior adult ministry will lead older persons to a greater sense of purpose in life. Although their physical vision may be dim, their spiritual vision can be sharp. With that sense of purpose, the self-esteem of older persons will be healthy.

Churches should recognize not only the importance of a sense of purpose in older adulthood but also the necessity of a healthy self-esteem.

Dr. E. W. Busse of Duke Medical Center says the key word for the older person is self-esteem.

Dr. Busse, one of the nation's leading gerontologists, has stated, "Our society, which has little appreciation for the non-achiever, must convince elderly that they are worthwhile and needed."

Productivity leads to positive self-esteem. Seniors must remain productive. Before retirement, an individual gained esteem by money, position, or accomplishment. Therefore, with these withdrawn, something must be found as a replacement. It is essential that our local churches provide programs for older adults that will build an atmosphere of creativity and belonging.

William Meninger has stated that "people who stay young despite their years do so because of an active interest that provides satisfaction through participation."

An active senior adult program will allow all senior adults to participate in active ministry through the local church.

General attitudes toward the older adult have changed greatly in the last several years. In 1872, a statement concerning a nursing home said: "In this home of refinement, Christian influence and comfort, relieved from toil and anxiety, older persons pleasantly spend the evening twilight of time, and serenely wait for the coming of their Lord." Over one hundred years have been required for this damaging attitude to begin to change.

A healthy philosophy toward older persons asserts that they are persons of worth, created in the image of God, whose lives never lose their purpose and meaning. Jesus' statement in John 10:10, "I am come that they might have life," is not negated when a person reaches sixty years of age.

Alexis Carrel wrote that "the aging man should neither stop working nor retire. Inactivity further impoverishes the content of time. Leisure impoverishes the content of time and is even more dangerous for the old than for the young. To those whose forces are declining appropriate work should be given. But not rest."

It is unfortunate that even now many people have not yet come to this way of thinking. A great deal still remains to be done in educating not only the general public but older persons themselves, who have been brought up to believe the traditional concept that to be old is to be exhausted and useless.

With growing awareness of independence for the elderly, churches must ask themselves what senior adults really want to make their lives more "abundant" and fulfilling.

The population at large has a practical stake in the effectiveness of the local church's senior adult ministry program, for participants in the program can affect the welfare of the community.

Programming for the elderly must be interpreted

not only to members of the community but also to older individuals themselves. Older adults, through active senior adult programs, are continuing to enjoy the "abundant life" that has no age barriers.

As novelist Paul Green has said, "The sun setting is no less beautiful than the sun rising."

Issue: Retirement and Evangelism Ideas

Gaines Dobbins has said, "If children are the best chance for Christ, then certainly senior adults are the last chance." Just because older adults have silver in their hair does not mean they have haloes on their heads.

Those who have conducted surveys in housing projects for the elderly have found great numbers of persons with no faith in God or relationship with a local church.

Why not train our senior adults to reach out to these lost individuals? We are missing an opportunity if we do not utilize our retirees, the greatest resource for evangelism in churches today. The Bible says that a Christian is to "bear fruit," no matter the age.

Of all people in our congregation, retirees have the spiritual reality of an active faith. They "know in whom they have believed" and can share a witness with a person from years of personal experience and walking with the Lord.

People need to hear the reality of the message. Senior adults have lived that reality. Not only should they be trained to witness to other senior adults but also to youth and young adults. We need to incorporate this untapped segment into existing visitation programs of churches.

Senior adults also have time to cultivate a witness. They can write letters, telephone, visit, send birthday cards, and even write witnessing letters. One of the things that they have learned over the years is how to care for one another. A lost person who knows that someone cares will listen.

Once a person accepts Christ as Lord the senior adults have time to disciple that new convert. They can encourage him in Bible study, help him with perplexing questions, make him feel a part of church programs.

In reaching other senior adults, regular club meetings can be a valid avenue. Unfortunately, many of our clubs are just "meet and eat" meetings.

If we will invite lost friends and neighbors to our meetings, we can interest them in attending our Sunday Schools.

Sunday School always has been the growth agent of any church. It is a fact that one out of three persons enrolled in Sunday School will make a profession of faith.

Arthur Flake asked: "What are churches for anyway? Are they not to carry out the will and complete work of Christ in the world? The soul-winning program of a church should be comprehensive enough to permit and encourage every member of the church and every organization of the church to participate."

As churches incorporate seniors into their visitation program, and clubs begin to encourage prospects to attend Sunday School, we will see a revival in senior adult evangelism, the mission of the church.

Issue: Retirement and Ministry Opportunities

The happiest people I know are those older adults who have lived a life dedicated to God, are continuing to serve others, and have a sense of ministry.

The writer of Proverbs says that "where there is no vision, the people perish" (29:18). It is essential that we maintain ministries or "visions" into retirement years if we are to find fulfillment.

Retirement years can be the most fulfilling of our lives, if we plan ahead. For those who fail to find their vocation in the senior years, retirement can be a prison. Ernest Hemingway, who committed suicide at age sixty-two, said that "to retire is the ugliest word in the English language." Instead of retiring to life, he retired from it.

To many adults it is not death they fear but life—a life of retirement with no sense of purposefulness.

There are many persons who have developed hobbies, second careers, or have become involved in volunteer service as God has given them their "vision."

Aging is a normal developmental phase of life. We

make the same transition to retirement that we have been making all our lives.

For the retired senior adult, satisfaction and abundant living come from continuing service to Jesus Christ, the greatest vocation of life.

The church is the largest institution in the world operated primarily by volunteers. Jesus said, "The Son of man came not to be ministered unto, but to minister" (Mark 10:45). "Inasmuch as ye have done it unto one of the least of these my brethren, ye have done it unto me" (Matt. 25:40). We are called to serve.

Service opportunities in churches abound for the older person. With retired persons comprising approximately 20 percent of our churches, older adults can be invaluable in serving others.

Service to others is a lifetime ministry. There is never a point in which we can "coast to glory." There is abundant joy from giving of ourselves to those around us.

After retirement at sixty-five, an increasing number of persons will have fifteen to thirty additional years to live. Studies have indicated that 80 to 85 percent are functionally healthy and able to do whatever they desire.

Senior adults have time and health to provide many hours of volunteer service through their churches. Certainly, senior adult ministry is not just a ministry to seniors but with and through them.

Seniors may serve in the community as well as

through local churches. Scripture tells us that we are to be a "light" unto others. How can we be that "light" if we are not involved in community programs?

According to the US Census Bureau, of 11.3 percent of the population over age sixty-five, 7 percent are providing some type of volunteer service.

Some places to serve in the community are: foster grandparents with over 14,000 persons in 182 projects; Retired Senior Volunteer Programs (RSVP) with over 230,000 persons working in courts, schools, libraries, and day-care centers in 680 projects; and Senior Companion Program with 1,900 persons in some 48 projects. These are just a few, but there are many other opportunities.

Within churches, there are many service opportunities. Even shut-ins may serve. I know a lady in my church living in a nursing home who calls her Sunday School classmates daily to check on their well-being.

David said that "they shall still bring forth fruit in old age" (Ps. 92:14). Senior adults want to remain productive in society, to "produce fruit."

They do not want leisuretime with nothing to do. They want opportunity to use their abilities, wisdom, and skills in serving others in the name of Christ.

Types of Service Opportunities

1. Seminar on nutrition

2. Learning activity songs that help with exercising

3. Cooperative gardening of vegetables or flowers

4. Organize sports

5. Low-cost meals at church

6. Drop-in center in some facility at the church building

7. Annual retreat for those who have recently lost a loved one by death

8. Help develop market outlets, cooperatives, and/or gift shop for crafts

9. Transportation to and from various places they need to go

10. Legal advice provided by attorneys at little or no charge

11. Help with taxes at little or no charge

12. Telephone assurance program

13. Working with stores and businesses to see about discounts for retirees

14. Delivery service for those who don't have means of hauling items

15. Crisis directory of services available in city

16. Meals on wheels

17. Visitation of shut-ins in homes or nursing homes

18. Daily or weekly radio program for 15 to 30 minutes designed for shut-ins (or television)

19. Develop a newsletter for retirees to be written, edited, printed, and distributed by retirees

20. Develop an informal center where retirees can call for various kinds of information

21. Develop a day-care center for aged persons who cannot be left alone during the day

22. Baby-sitting for young adult group in the church to assist them in their ministry activities for their own group

23. Help homebound adults with study of the Sunday School lesson

24. Form a group who will sit with people in hospitals or who will sit with families during surgery of family members

25. Open home to college dormitory students or military personnel so they can have a homelike atmosphere for visiting with friends

26. Help teach poor people how to plan and cook budget meals

27. Take groups of children shopping

28. Hospital volunteer services

29. Establish a check-out service for equipment such as: hospital beds, wheelchairs, walking canes, TV sets, radios, cassette tape recorders and players

30. Visiting newcomers to the community and inviting them to church

Issue: The Frail Elderly

Although the elderly have many and varied needs, the most critical ones which can lead to other problems are usually physical in nature. The longer a person lives, the more opportunity he has to be damaged physically.

This can even progress to the point of causing social and emotional problems. A church ministry should consider physiological needs of the older adult.

Many needs of the elderly could be better comprehended if we understood the loss of sensory perception of the aged.

With passage of time, a stronger external stimulus is required to trigger sensory response. But a one-to-one relationship does not necessarily exist between the amount of loss and behavioral consequences.

The elderly compensate by various methods—for instance, by extending arms while reading the paper, putting on hearing aids, increasing illumination in a dark room, and just paying better attention.

Although their vision may be deteriorating, older persons often check on what they are doing with their body parts just by looking at them; they must have this additional signal to let them know exactly where that hand or foot is.

These are positive adjustments which help to compensate for loss in visual acuity. But the psychological need that can develop as a result of such a loss is devastating.

A lifetime of an individual's habits has been based on 20/20 vision. If information is received partially or incorrectly, he may make mistakes, and this, in time, makes him become hesitant. He then begins to lose confidence in himself.

Sometimes older persons will deny a sensory loss. By not hearing conversation, for example, they may withdraw and then think that other people are making no effort to include them, or even that they are being excluded. They feel that they are left out of things; consequently they become so.

In its programming ministry the church should be sure to make itself understood by the elderly, as well as to understand physiological changes occurring in them. The church must let the elderly know that they are a part of the whole.

In formulating programming for the elderly, churches must also understand that older persons typically experience a loss of strength and agility. Perhaps the most impressive change in response is the slowing process.

Reaction time in human beings begins to slow shortly after the age of twenty. Writing is slowed with age. Pressuring a person to speed up tends to make him slower and more prone to make errors.

If the task cannot be completed in a certain amount of time, the older person seems to lose grasp of the instructions, and he may not complete the task at all. Thus, if a church employs older volunteers to direct its activities, it must be understood that they need adequate time for preparation of the task.

Although the focus in this section has been on some physiological needs of the frail elderly, other basic needs of older adults are no less important. Health, security, love, esteem, and self-fulfillment are concerns for all of life.

Ministry ideas with the frail elderly could include:

1. Cooperative buying of food items
2. Handyman services to help elderly maintain their own homes
3. Provide information upon request for types of housing the elderly may be forced to live in.
4. Meals on Wheels Program
5. Home delivery of services with food items, etc.
6. Trained individuals who will go into the homes of the homebound to lead a meaningful worship service.
7. Volunteers who will take the frail elderly shopping for commodity foods, to the doctor and dentist, or to visit friends.
8. Provide volunteers social service, and legal advice consultants for the elderly.

Issue: Ageism in the Church

What is ageism? Have you ever heard someone refer to a senior adult as inflexible, cranky, or senile? The general tendency is to accept such remarks with little or no thought. These statements may be made by youth, children of aging parents, and even senior adults. Often, these remarks act as self-fulfilling prophecies. Older persons hear the ageist remarks and feel they must assume those rigid attitudes or behaviors because they are "supposed" to.

The term "ageism" was coined in 1968 by Robert Butler, nationally recognized gerontologist. Ageism represents a basically prejudicial orientation toward a particular segment of society based upon misconceptions, half-truths, apathy, and ignorance. It has as its foundation the belief that the older segment of our society is fundamentally different from all other segments and, by inference, is inferior.

Four factors should be considered when trying to understand origins of prejudicial attitudes about the aged. These factors are: attitude toward youth, limited contact with elderly, the media, and ignorance.

1. Ours is basically a youth-oriented society. We tend to glorify youth by placing great value on being young. We attempt to maintain our youthfulness regardless of cost. By placing such emphasis upon youth, society is saying two things: youth is good, and old is bad.

2. Limited contact with the elderly is a second factor that creates ageism. Few people in our society have personal contact with the elderly for any extended period of time. Grandparents or parents may be visited only on rare occasions, after living many miles apart.

Those who have little contact with members of a particular group are more likely to accept whatever myths or stereotypes society places on them.

3. A third factor creating ageism is often the media. To a great extent, television, movies, and literature are responsible for creating myths about aging.

Relatively few older persons (besides George Burns) are featured on television or the movies. Often, when they are portrayed, they are presented in the typical stereotypical manner that reinforces the myths that they are forgetful, behaving foolishly, easily outwitted, or without power or status. At the other extreme, they are presented as all-knowing, all-good, and all-wise. Neither portrait accurately depicts any human being.

4. The fourth factor creating ageism is ignorance. Until recently, little information about the process of aging was available.

As the proportion of older persons increases, so does research in the field of aging. As this information is published and persons educated, many myths will dissolve.

Churches need to recognize and affirm older adults by refusing to accept aging stereotypes. Ageist attitudes will diminish as we recognize worth, talents, and abilities of senior adults on their own merits, not preconceived myths.

The local church can dispel ageist attitudes by providing more age-integrated programming. Here are some examples of age-integrated ministry:

1. A monthly recreation time at the church where an evening of crafts, hobbies, or table games could be enjoyed by all age groups.

2. One-day trips to interesting historical sites, state parks, zoo, or museums.

3. Workday ministries where all age groups "blitz"

a homebound person's home to trim, mow, rake, wash, paint, clean, or provide other services needed to spruce up the home.

4. Churchwide banquets where all age groups are encouraged to participate.

5
Club Programming Suggestions

Club Programming Suggestions

Variety is the mother of Enjoyment.
                    —Benjamin Disraeli

Much of the success of the senior adult regular club meetings is due to the variety of programming we plan. By just looking at the yellow pages, we can see numerous possibilities for programming. We can also contact other organizations which have regular meetings and glean suggestions from the program chairperson.

Keepsake Day
Ask each member of your senior adult group to bring a keepsake that he or she has treasured over the years. Display all the items with the owner's name by each. Give awards or other recognition for "the oldest," "the most unusual," and so forth. Ask the pastor to attend the meeting to judge the entries.

Picture Day
Have the senior adults bring pictures of themselves which are at least thirty-five years old and place them on a bulletin board. Grant a prize to the senior who recognizes the most persons. Have all seniors participating to tell something about the

background of the photo: when it was taken and what was happening in the world at the time.

Remember When

Have discussions about "Remember When." Some possible topics could be: "How the City Has Changed," "Cures My Grandmother Knew," "Did the 'Good Ole Times' Ever Exist?" "The Coldest Winter I Remember," and so forth.

Golden Oldies

Periodically check out from the library or rent an early "talkies" for the group to watch. Serve popcorn, soft drinks, and have some great laughs. Discuss the days of Greta Garbo or John Barrymore. Have a local librarian come and give a brief introduction of the background and stars of the film.

Meet the Mayor

The older adults of our churches and communities comprise a large percentage of the voting population. In order to keep your senior adults abreast of political events and issues, invite the mayor of your city to your club meeting for an informal meeting. You may wish to also invite two or three other churches to join you for this dialogue exchange.

It would be important not to use this occasion to intimidate the mayor. Keep the meeting apolitical. Ask questions regarding the operation of the city government, city growth projections, services for senior citizens, legislation affecting older adults, and other pertinent questions.

If the mayor is unavailable in your city, perhaps he could send one of his assistants as his representative.

For decorations, small American flags could center each table. (A state flag could be obtained from the mayor's office.) As a part of the program, it would be appropriate to have the pledge of allegiance to the American flag.

For a devotional theme, Romans 13:1 would be appropriate: "Let every soul be subject unto the higher powers. For there is no power but of God: the powers that be are ordained of God."

Christmas Shopping

Christmas is a time for sharing and giving. Although many older adults are on fixed incomes, they still want to share with others during this important time of the year.

For the program, invite several representatives from large department stores in the area. Ask them to share information concerning the merchandise available and dates of upcoming sales. These persons may also know about some senior citizen discounts that your members may not be familiar with. The representatives may also share some ideas for gifts costing under ten dollars. This information will aid the older adult in what to shop for, when to shop for it, and discount opportunities that may be available.

As a ministry of the club, encourage your active

senior adults to take the names and addresses of two homebound persons they can help with shopping. We often forget that the homebound enjoy giving gifts as well as anyone else. Their unique problem is that they must get someone else to shop for them. They will greatly appreciate this service.

Armchair Tour of Hawaii

One of the enjoyments of retirement is the ability to travel. Yet, for many, a trip to Hawaii is out of the question. This armchair tour could fit everyone's budget.

The key to the success of this meeting is the change of environment. Psychologists say that a change in one's environment is stimulating to the senses. Turn the meeting place into a tropical paradise. Bring in artificial plants, flowers, leis for everyone, Hawaiian music, and Hawaiian food for lunch—make it an indoor luau.

For the program, contact the regional library and check out a 16-mm film on Hawaii. Ask your associational missionary to do some research, and after the film present to the group what Southern Baptist churches are doing to minister to the islanders as well as tourists who visit Hawaii.

In order to incorporate intergenerational programming, have one of the young adult classes sponsor this armchair tour. You may even have someone in your church who has been to Hawaii and can teach the meaning and message of the hula.

Make a special effort to transport your homebound to this event. Many of them will never have seen anything quite like an armchair tour of Hawaii.

Energy Conservation

With the high cost of energy, conservation is essential for most older persons. There are many ways in which senior adults can conserve. Contact your local power and light company and ask them to send a representative to tell your group about some of these energy-saving methods.

There may also be a handyman service for senior adults in your area. This may be a church-sponsored organization or a community agency that does repair work for the elderly. As the power and light representative makes suggestions on how to conserve energy, the handyman could make his services available to those at this meeting. The purpose of merging the two program personalities is to make possible to the group the means to accomplish the energy-saving changes in their homes.

For a devotional thought, you could use Philippians 4:5, "Let your moderation be known unto all men." We are to be moderate in all things—even in the use of energy, which is costly as well as a dwindling natural resource.

Share a Craft/Hobby

Many older persons find great satisfaction in craft work. Men and women have taken up fulfilling and even profitable craft hobbies in the retirement years. Anyone senses accomplishment as she creates a beautiful object from raw material.

Many senior adults have yet to discover this joy. Promote this meeting for everyone to bring a craft or hobby and share with the group how they developed the interest. Your group will have an excellent opportunity to encourage those not involved in crafts to find a hobby.

In addition, have a hobby-craft expert to come and share the enormous number of low-cost crafts and material that can be purchased.

As a follow-up, form a monthly craft group. This could be a ceramics class, quilting bee, sewing shrimp nets, whatever the interest of the group. Whatever the craft, have a purpose in its creation. Give the items to an orphanage as a gift or shower shut-ins at Christmas. There is even more contentment as we give to others the fruits of our labor.

Victory Gardens

Gerontologists state that one of the primary needs of older adults is proper diet or nutrition. Contact the county hospital and ask their nutritionist to come and discuss the importance of proper diet in older adulthood. They can bring pamphlets, slides, and other materials to distribute.

As an addition to the program, discuss the "victory gardens" which were advocated and popular during

the great depression. Ask who had a "victory garden" and what vegetables they raised.

To follow up, encourage the adults to plant a vege-
table garden. Have one of the farmers in the church
plan with the group the process, or steps, in planting.
Not only will this provide some moderate exercise,
but the vegetables harvested can be of benefit to
their nutritional needs.

Discount Community Savings

According to a survey conducted by Duke University, inadequate income was ranked number one as
the major problem confronting the aged. Many older
persons are on a fixed, limited income.

Two months before the meeting, organize a committee to research all discounts and services available
in the community. Have them contact Senior Citizens, Social Security, the Area Agency on Aging, and
all other organizations that serve senior adults and
find out what discounts are available.

One of the greatest needs of most community
organizations serving the elderly is the promotion of
those savings or services for the aged. Have the committee share with the group the information they
have found. This could be put into a written form and
distributed to all senior adults in the church.

This committee could be responsible for regular
reporting of community savings, keeping the senior
adult informed.

To keep the senior adult informed on a regular

basis, have the committee make quarterly reports of community savings that are available.

Public Library Service

If we are to fulfill one potential as senior adults, continuing education is essential. To be productive in the church and society, we must be informed as to national and local issues and how they affect us. Local public libraries offer a milieu of programs for senior adults to help them maintain that awareness.

Those who are handicapped visually could take advantage of "talking books" on cassettes or records. This service can be utilized also if the person has difficulty holding books. There are also programs offered on "Taxes" and "Handicaps." Large-print books and magazines are also in stock. There are reading clubs, discussion groups, and family films. Most libraries will have a film collection pertaining to aging.

To conclude your meeting have the representative bring a film and lead a brief discussion following the showing. A good film for discussion would be *The Transformation of Mabel Wells.*

Following the program, the group could organize a reading club which would meet monthly or weekly to discuss books written for senior adults.

Cooking for One

The President's Task Force on Aging has stated that the nutritional needs of older adults is a major factor for good health. Many widowed persons do not take the time to eat or plan well-balanced meals. In examining the incidence of malnutrition among the elderly, insufficient income was only one of several causes. Other reasons are inadequate transportation to get to the store, the chronically ill older person unable to prepare a hot meal, and misinformation on the importance of a balanced diet.

Invite the county nutritionist to present a program on the necessity of a proper diet with examples of menus designed for cooking for one person. Be sure that widowed men as well as the single, never married, are included in this program. As an offshoot of the program, a weekly cooking class could be organized for the single older person.

For a devotional theme, discuss what the Bible says concerning taking care of the body (1 Cor. 3:16). Proper nutritional habits are essential for a healthy body.

Patriotic Concert

Contact the local symphony about conducting a concert for your church or associational senior adults several months in advance. Since summer months are usually slower, several groups in your area could combine their club meeting for this concert. Most symphonies would be willing to perform for such an event. If contacted ahead of time, they may be able to play requests.

The key to the success of this meeting is advance

publicity and planning. Transportation would need to be provided to the concert hall or theater. After the concert, lunch could be planned at one of the local restaurants. They would need to be contacted ahead of time for adequate seating and possible menu selection. It would be appropriate to invite the symphony members to lunch with you. This would give the senior adults opportunity to ask questions and converse with the members.

As you conclude the luncheon, an appropriate devotional reading would be Psalm 150.

Watermelon Party

The greatest thing in the heat of the summer is the availability of cool, sweet watermelons. Contact a local grower and plan to have for this meeting a "Watermelon Party."

Since grandchildren are out of school, this would be a good time to invite them to one of our meetings. Several times a year, it would be good to include grandchildren in various activities. They need to see that their grandparents can have as good a time as they can.

In conjunction with the party, it would be good to organize art/craft demonstrations and displays. Set up colorful booths for display of various crafts and handwork. Some of the seniors could even give demonstrations of their art. Quilting, weaving, and sculpturing—to name a few—are always of particular interest.

This display would be fascinating to the grandchildren in attendance. Some of the grandparents could even instruct them as to how they create their art. It could be a learning experience for both senior adults and grandchildren.

Fourth of July Celebration

This patriotic meeting should be the highlight of the month. Senior adults are one of the most patriotic groups in America. They have a higher turnout of registered voters than any other age group.

Plan an outdoor meeting if possible. Let someone be responsible for the planning of games such as horseshoes, croquet, and other lawn games. The ladies would enjoy these games as much as the men. Homemade ice cream is a favorite, and July is a good time to bring out the churns. A covered-dish picnic would be the meal for the day. The tables could be decorated with red, white, and blue streamers, liberty bells, and stars. The setting should be very relaxed and informal.

For this special occasion, contact four associational ministers of music to present a concert of patriotic music. At the close of the picnic, a minifireworks display would be an exciting conclusion. Contact your local fire department for information on the fireworks display.

As a benediction, have everyone join hands in a circle and sing "God Bless America."

Table Game Tournaments

Begin promoting this meeting about three months in advance. Let this be an annual tradition of the "Table Game Olympics."

Everyone enjoys the competition of table games. Announce what games will be played and encourage the seniors to practice for the "Olympics." Invite the mayor of the city to come and award the ribbons or trophies to the winners of each game. Any book of games will have numerous table games to choose from.

As an added feature, challenge another church senior adult club to participate in the tournaments. This could also be an associational event with the winner holding the "Olympics Banner" until the next tournament.

This type of competition is healthy and stimulating to the mind. Encourage all your seniors to participate.

Writing for Fun

For this program, invite a retired English teacher to come and discuss the importance of putting our thoughts and experiences of life in writing. Many older persons are afraid of writing, but it can bring great joy.

As a project, have the senior adults in the club and church write a devotional book for use by the entire congregation. If you do not have enough senior adults to write for one year, write a devotional booklet for the Christmas or Easter season. Not only will this be a way for senior adults to express themselves in writing, but they are sharing a personal experience with Jesus Christ with their children, grandchildren, and church.

At this meeting, have everyone begin to write their devotional thoughts. Have them think of a Scripture and write why this Scripture is meaningful to them. They may want to write about when they became a Christian and how their life has changed.

Their writing will not only be enjoyable but inspirational as well.

Preview of Senior Adult Chautauquas

Last year over nine thousand persons registered for the Chautauqua at Ridgecrest and Glorieta. This annual Southern Baptist event is growing each year as more seniors become aware of this spiritually uplifting week.

To preview the Chautauqua, show slides of Ridgecrest or Glorieta that you or a friend may have. Plan a full day "Mini-Chautauqua" at your church. Give all the club senior adults a sample of what occurs daily.

Find a brochure of last year's event and plan a similar one-day schedule. Begin with a morning watch, then have breakfast at the church. After breakfast invite the pastor or a local minister to conduct a Bible study. When the study is over, have an exercise class or other activity and then conclude with lunch.

After lunch, encourage all your seniors to attend the October Chautauqua. Have all information and reservation forms available. This one-day preview will give them a sampling of Chautauqua.

Senior Adult Conference

In conjunction with Senior Adult Day, why not have a Senior Adult Conference Monday through Wednesday? A committee could be chosen to plan the three-day event. Invite a specialist in aging ministry to conduct the three-day conference. Three months before the date of the conference conduct a survey at the regular club meeting to determine the topics to be studied. Some potential courses could be: continuing growth opportunities, what the Bible says about aging, adapting to a changing environment, intergenerational experience, developing friendships, evangelism, and many other subjects. A list could be compiled, and seniors could check five or six of those listed that would be of special interest to them.

After determining the topics, elect a steering committee to plan the three-day conference.

An innovative plan would be to invite all young people to a banquet on Monday evening.

Where Is My Place?

President Ronald Reagan has said that retirees make up the largest percentage of volunteers in America and need to be utilized not only in the private sector but in the church as well.

Invite the pastor and all staff members to come share with the club some of the volunteer ministry opportunities offered through the church. Senior adults can offer an invaluable service to the church if they know where they can fit in. After all staff members have explained the possibilities, conduct a Christian Service Survey to give them an opportunity to actually volunteer for service.

It is a myth that older persons want to sit and rock their retirement years away. Any healthy, older adult desires to continue serving as an expression of his growing faith.

There are also many opportunities to serve in the local Baptist Association as well as community programs.

In Appreciation . . .

Sunday School continues to be the growth agent of local churches. Our Sunday School teachers of the Senior Adult departments are persons earnest in their desire to teach the saved and reach out to the lost. It would be appropriate once a year to conduct a special appreciation dinner for all teachers, officers, and department officers of the church. The pastor could be invited to speak concerning the importance of Sunday School in the overall senior adult program.

A certificate of appreciation could be given to each teacher and officer to express the group's gratitude for the time dedicated to teaching. A corsage could be presented to the ladies as they arrive.

It is important to "give the roses" while a person is living. Many of our teachers have given years of service through the Sunday School. They have prayed for and encouraged many persons, and it would be appropriate to honor them on this Appreciation Day.

Housing Options

A major concern for many senior adults is that of housing. The economic facts of life explain why this is such a desperate concern. Older adults want to maintain independent living for as long as possible. Yet they need to be aware of all housing alternatives.

Invite administrators or managers of as many housing models from the community as feasible. Form a panel of these individuals and ask your senior adults to be prepared to ask questions. Have the managers describe their housing alternative before a question-and-answer period. Be sure to have represented the four basic living arrangements: independent living, congregate housing, limited medical care, and long-term care facilities.

Some of the housing subjects to be covered should be: sheltered housing, nursing homes, foster homes for adults, SRO (single room occupancy) hotels, group homes, and joint households.

The cost of each one of these models should also be explained since some retirement housing can be quite expensive.

Grandchildren's Day

Have the senior adults bring one of their grandchildren or great-grandchildren to the group meeting. If some older adults cannot bring grandchildren, have them bring pictures and one of their grandchildren's favorite toys, craft exhibits, or a special gift the senior adult received from the grandchild. There may be older adults with no grandchildren; have them bring a great-niece or nephew.

Intergenerational programming is essential for the normal growth of any church. Take this opportunity to introduce your grandchild to your friends. Show pictures, crafts, and so forth, to all attending. The grandchild will gain a new appreciation for the grandparent as he or she relates to peers. Have some activity games to involve the children and senior adults. For the program have the pastor or a staff person to share a positive message on older adults relating to youth, and how youth can be more involved with older adults.

Social Security Update

To maintain a balance in programming, informational as well as entertaining subjects should be covered. The subject of Social Security generally elicits a myriad of stated opinions when mentioned to older adults. One of the reasons is the confusion as to the future of Social Security.

In order to inform and, therefore, lessen some of the fears about Social Security, contact the local district manager of the Social Security Administration and ask him or her to address the group at a future date. Promote this an an informal question-and-answer forum. Have senior adults think of questions to ask and write them down to be submitted at the meeting. The district manager will appreciate having this opportunity to dispel the many myths of Social Security. The manager would have already heard many of these concerns from prior meetings with older persons.

In conjunction with this meeting, a representative of American Association of Retired Persons (AARP) could be invited to share what the AARP lobbyist in Washington is doing regarding advocacy and Social Security. The AARP national organization has a full-time lobbyist to represent aging issues. The representative would be aware of present action being taken in regard to Social Security questions.

New Year Expectations

We have all heard, "Plan your work, and work your plan." It is important for everyone to have goals, to set objectives, and to sense a purpose in all they are doing.

Take the first meeting of the New Year to share the ministries, activities, and special events of the coming year. Prior to the meeting, the Senior Adult Council would have met and planned events around the needs and interests of the senior group. Remember, this is not a ministry *to* but *with* senior adults.

An overarching theme for the New Year could be shared, with all activities as a "spoke" to this "hub." If the church has an annual emphasis, the senior adults could support the theme with their programming.

As you begin to discuss dates for various activities, give each senior a calendar, so they may mark it and keep it at home to remind them of future events. Some of the dates to be marked could be travel opportunities, group-meeting programs, special banquets and themes, and the setting of a date for Senior Adult Day in the church.

The senior adult will appreciate knowing in advance what's going on. To complement the program, a brochure could be distributed with activities and dates already printed.

RESOURCES

Kerr, Horace. *How to Minister to Senior Adults in Your Church*. Nashville: Broadman Press, 1980.

Sessoms, Robert. *150 Ideas for Activities with Senior Adults*. Nashville: Broadman Press, 1977.

Sessoms, Bob and Carolyn. *52 Complete Recreation*

Programs for Senior Adults. Nashville: Convention Press, 1979.

Vickery, Florence. *Creative Programming for Older Adults.* New York: Associate Press, 1972.

6
Ideas and Activities

Exercise in the Senior Adult Years

The benefits of proper exercise can be enjoyed throughout the life span. Richard B. Couey, author of *Lifelong Fitness and Fulfillment,* says: "Maintaining health and strength are important parts of Christian stewardship, for the Bible calls our bodies temples of God." It is good stewardship to care for our bodies. Preventive maintenance is always better in the long run. One of the activity components under Services Needed (see *How to Minister to Senior Adults in Your Church,* Kerr) that a senior adult ministry could implement would be an exercise class for senior adults.

Older adults, as well as other age groups, need to increase their heart rates and maintain that rate for a period of time. This is called cardiovascular endurance. By increasing the number of beats per minute, the heart becomes more like a machine and works more efficiently. When the heart beats more times per minute, the blood circulation increases to all parts of the body. By gradually increasing the amount and length of physical activity the progress of endurance becomes greater.

One of the factors which has led to a steady increase in the average life expectancy has been the rediscovery of the importance of regular exercise and proper nutrition.

Suggested Activity Component: Exercise Class

1. Before beginning any exercise program get clearance from a doctor.

2. The exercise leader should try to attend a workshop that gives guidance in this type of activity.

3. The exercise leader must be aware of the limitations of each participant.

4. The leader should maintain a simple routine and keep the number of repetitions low until he has a feel for the fitness level of the group.

5. The exercise leader should safety-check the equipment and exercise area that is to be used.

6. After a few weeks the leader might divide the class into skill levels to include new participants at an entry level.

7. It is a good idea to have a nutrition specialist help the participants with their diets to make the class a complete fitness approach.

8. The purpose of the program should be to increase the range of motion in the joints, expand the lungs and breathing system, and develop additional muscle tone and strength.

Resources

Couey, Richard. *Lifelong Fitness and Fulfillment.* Nashville: Broadman Press, 1980.

Church Recreation Magazine, July, August, September 1976.

American Association of Retired Persons. *Pep Up Your Life.* PF 3248 (484).

"Exercise Can Keep People Alive Longer." *USA Today,* August 21, 1984.

Administration on Aging. *The Fitness Challenge.* Washington, DC.

Film: *Active People Over 60 and Basic Exercise for People Over 60.* North Texas State University Gerontology Film Collection, Denton, Texas.

Intergenerational Activities

It is unfortunate that our society and even some churches are becoming age segregated. The philosophy of the "Me" generation has crept into all age groups. The result of age segregation is that many of our youth have limited contact with senior adults and senior adults with the young.

Lack of intergenerational ministry between persons of different ages is of particular concern because children's attitudes about growing older develop early in life. Most images are drawn from what they see presented by the media. Studies have shown that older adults appear in only 4 percent of prime-time television programs. When they are portrayed, they are usually pictured as incompetent.

A study by the University of Maryland Center on Aging showed that only 16 percent of a sampling of 549 children's books portrayed older characters as significant.

Churches developing intergenerational ministries is an excellent way to counteract negative stereotypes about growing older. Such ministry encourages young people to interact with older adults and to develop love for and trust in older persons. Being with young people who are enthusiastic about life is, in turn, good for older adults.

Intergenerational ministry is more than cookies and choruses once a month. It's the developing of continuing life-changing relationships between young people and their older friends. This ministry can range from simple ongoing visitation programs to detailed weekend work projects.

One of the benefits is the love that develops between the youth and the senior adults. These friendships often continue for many years, and each age group learns and benefits from the other.

Resources

Backes, Greg. *Age Isn't Really Important.* Harrisburg: Backes Music, 1983 (an intergenerational musical).

Center for Studies in Aging. *Gerontological Film*

Collection. North Texas State University, Box 13438, NT Station, Denton, TX 76203 (films and slides available on intergenerational needs and programs).

Howell, John. *Senior Adult Family Life.* Nashville: Broadman Press, 1979.

Youth Conferences with Older Americans (program). AARP, Program Development Section, 1909 K Street, NW, Washington, DC 20049.

Help for Adult Children with Frail Parents

Margaret M. Heckler, former secretary of the Department of Health and Human Services, stated in her annual report to the nation that life expectancy increased again last year to an average 74.7 years. This is a full year's increase since 1980. The implications of this for local church ministry are staggering and challenging.

Due to increased average life expectancy, a new phenomenon occurring in the United States is the growing number of retirees caring for older parents. Two of the needs of these caregivers are: information on community services available to them and emotional support during this stage of their lives.

Component Activity

Under the category of services needed, an activity component of your senior adult ministry could be establishment of a "Support Program for Adult Children." This group, made up of children of frail, aging parents could meet regularly for information and emotional support.

Informational

Some resources for information available in your community for caregivers are: the local Red Cross chapter, physicians, senior centers, health departments, and your area agency on aging.

Offices on Aging: There are 50 state, 667 area, and 25,000 local offices on aging. To find one in your area, call the United States Government or state government offices on aging listed in the phone book. Ask what services are available in your area to assist your aging parent(s) to maintain independence in their home or yours. Also inquire about existing support groups.

Support Group

The planning guide published by AARP entitled "Hand in Hand: Learning from and Caring for Older Parents" is an excellent guide in developing the needed ministry. Adult children need to group together to share experiences. Knowing you are not alone means a great deal. (For additional information contact: Senior Adult Consultant, The Baptist Sunday School Board, 127 Ninth Avenue, North, Nashville, TN 37234.)

Resources

Bressler, Dawn S. *Hand in Hand: Learning from and Caring for Older Parents.* AARP, 1909 K Street NW, Washington, DC 20049, 1984.

Cook, Gary. *Counseling with . . . Persons Caring for Aging Parents.* Baptist General Convention of Texas, Christian Life Commission, 703 North Ervay Street, Dallas, Texas 75201; attention: Mike Lundy.

Howse, W. L., III. "You and Your Aging Parent." *Home Life,* November 1981, pp. 13-15.

Schwartz, Arthur N. *Survival Handbook for Children of Aging Parents.* Chicago: Follet, 1977.

Newsletter

Change, Newsletter of the National Support Center for Families of the Aging. P.O. Box 245, Swarthmore, PA 19081.

Film

My Mother, My Father. Terra Nova Films, Inc., 9848 S. Winchester Avenue, Chicago, IL 60643; phone 312/881-8491.

Evangelism and Senior Adults

One of the most neglected areas in present church ministry with senior adults is evangelism. We often take for granted that because a person has reached age sixty-five he or she automatically inherits the

Kingdom. Many senior adults have not accepted Jesus Christ as their Lord. A balanced Senior Adult Ministry will seek ways to develop evangelism programs utilizing senior adults to reach these persons.

If we are to reach the world for Jesus Christ through Bold Mission Thrust, we must utilize the gifts and skills of our senior adults. Approximately 20 percent of the Southern Baptist Convention membership is age sixty or over. Are we including them in our evangelism programs? Of all the adults in our churches, they have the spiritual reality of an active faith. They also have the time to cultivate a witness through the local church as well as the time to disciple or nurture a new Christian as that person begins his/her spiritual journey.

The latest demographics indicate that 11.3 percent of our population (more than 25 million) is over age sixty-five. What are we doing to train our senior adults to reach this growing number of retirees?

The Sunday School is still the growth agent of our churches. One out of three persons enrolled in Sunday School will make a profession of faith. Arthur Flake once said, "What are churches for anyway? Are they not to carry out the will and complete work of Christ in the world? The soul-winning program of a church should be comprehensive enough to permit and encourage every member of the church and every organization of the church to participate."

Are we encouraging our senior adults and our senior adult clubs to carry on the soul-winning mission of the church? Let's think about it.

Ways to Cultivate a Witness with Senior Adults

1. Invite unchurched visitors at your regular club meetings to attend Sunday School.

2. Visit the unchurched and take an adult quarterly, senior adult newsletter, and the church bulletin.

3. Organize an evangelism training class on reaching unchurched senior adults.

4. Offer to bring unchurched persons to Sunday School and/or church.

5. Meet for lunch or dinner.

6. Telephone and invite to a special activity.

7. Use tracts during visits.

8. Discuss what it means to be a Christian.

9. Write a witnessing letter.

10. Be available to minister during periods of bereavement or need.

Telephone Reassurance

It has been estimated that seven million older adults live alone. For many of these individuals a daily telephone call could mean the difference between life and death. This ministry through a local church provides the homebound with a concerned volunteer caller daily and the assurance that they will receive immediate medical assistance if they are incapacitated.

The ministry could be developed under any number of possible names, but a telephone reassurance ministry would locate the isolated, frail elderly in a community and enlist volunteers to make a daily telephone call at a prearranged time. If the individual does not respond to the call, an emergency procedure is put into effect by calling a friend, neighbor, or even the police. These individuals will have a key to enter the home and check to see if the elderly person is safe.

This ministry will provide a check on the daily well-being of the elderly, and it could also serve as an information service for the individuals served. Referrals to local aging organizations and agencies would be greatly appreciated. The church also needs to determine if they will offer temporary use of the ministry, when for instance, the adult children of an older person go on vacation for a few weeks during the summer. This would alleviate any fears the children may have in leaving a frail parent behind.

Resources

Virginia Rogers. *Guidelines for a Telephone Reassurance Service.* Ann Arbor, Mich: Institute of Gerontology, The University of Michigan.

American Association of Retired Persons (AARP), 1909 K Street, NW, Washington, DC 20049.

Offer Budget Service for the Elderly, Aging in Michigan, Michigan Commission on Aging, Department of Social Services, 1101 South Washington Avenue, Lansing, Mich.

Social Services Day

One of the goals of a service adult program should be to work with social service agencies in the community in providing adequate care for seniors. Once a year have a number of speakers from various social agencies come to the church and give ten-minute talks explaining their services for older persons and how to access them. The planning committee could set up booths for each agency so that after the program representatives could counsel with those interested. Some examples of agencies to include would be: Senior Citizens, Inc., Social Security Administration, Legal Services, Arthritis Foundation, Consumer Affairs Department, Area Agency on Aging, housing authority, and so forth.

At this time a social service consultant could be elected to the Senior Adult Council to be on call to the seniors with questions. Often, when services are needed, older persons do not know who to call or if they should call. This designated person could provide an invaluable service to senior adults.

Resource

Area Agency on Aging

Senior Day-Care Centers

A day-care center is a place where frail senior adults come during the day and then return home at night. It may be a day club or a workshop or even a day hospital.

There would be a variety of activities planned to coincide with the energy levels and abilities of the senior adult.

Many churches are not using many of their church plant facilities and may have a room or rooms which could be converted to a day-care program.

For those involved in the program, the advantages are many: continued contact with other people, a sense of getting out into the community.

This service is also a tremendous help to families who care for their parent(s) at home. If only for a couple of days a week, it gives the family some time to get out of the house and to take care of routine tasks.

Any church, small or large, can implement this program as a ministry for frail senior adults in the church and community.

Resources

Local Area Agency on Aging

Public Information Specialists, HCFA/DHHS, 330 Independence Avenue, SW, Washington, DC 20201.

Service Opportunities

One of the five content areas (spiritual enrichment, socialization, learning opportunities, service opportunities, service needs) in developing a balanced senior adult ministry is service opportunities—areas in which senior adults can do volunteer ministry.

It is clear that retirees do not want increased leisuretime with nothing to do. They want the opportunity to use their abilities, wisdom, and skills in serving others in the name of Christ.

Volunteer Service Corps

Under the content area of service opportunities, why not establish an activity component entitled Volunteer Service Corps? This corps would need a committee and a chairperson to find opportunities of service in the church and the community. They would need to recruit volunteers, train them, and provide them with meaningful service opportunities. This corps should have a separate training program for interested persons and be recognized at a special banquet each year.

Suggested Service Opportunities

1. Develop an evangelistic outreach program to contact retirees with no church affiliation.

2. Visit new residents in the community and invite them to club meetings and church services.

3. Make scrapbooks for homebound persons.

4. Provide a reading program for the visually impaired.

5. Consider hospital volunteer services.

6. Shop for the homebound.

7. Distribute toys to needy children at Christmas.

8. Deliver Meals-on-Wheels.

9. Visit nursing-home residents.

10. Provide transportation.

11. Give telephone reassurance.

12. Develop a retiree information hot line.

13. Provide day care for older persons.

14. Develop a tape ministry through the church.

Resources for Older Volunteers

Home Mission Board. Christian Social Ministries, 1350 Spring Street, NW, Atlanta, GA 30309; 404/873-4041.

Opportunities Include: Campers on Mission, Christian Service Corps (CSC), Lay Renewal, and Mission Service Corps.

Foreign Mission Board, 3806 Monument Avenue, Richmond, VA 23230; 804/353-0151.

Opportunities Include: English Language Baptist Church, Medical-Dental Volunteer Program, Missionary Associate, Relief and Disaster Response, Volunteer Evangelistic Efforts, and Volunteer Involvement in Missions.

Community Clown Ministry

An innovative ministry today which is growing in churches and senior adult groups is "clowning." Clowning touches the lives of persons by making them laugh. Laughter is healing, for both the giver and receiver.

This is an excellent intergenerational tool of ministry that can cross every age barrier: preschoolers, children, youth, young and median adults.

The senior adult "clown" visits child day cares, nursing homes, orphanages, hospitals, or any other place people congregate. They talk, listen, share themselves, and give a tender touch or dry a tear. Senior "clowns" have tremendous success at breaking down barriers.

This is an excellent component ministry which overlaps socialization for the senior and service opportunities.

Resources

Robertson, Everett. *The Ministry of Clowning.* Nashville: Broadman Press, 1983.

Hartish, Karl. *Introduction to Clowning.* Baltimore, MD, 1973.

McVicar, Wes. *Clown Omnibus.* New York: Association Press.

The Mark of the Clown (movie). Mass Media Ministries, 2116 North Charles Street, Baltimore, MD 21218.

Crime Prevention Class

Crime prevention is a major concern to many of our older adults who are living in rapidly changing neighborhoods. In a 1975 Harris Poll, senior adults said that crime and the fear of crime are their most serious problems. Making the home or apartment secure by practicing some crime prevention techniques is one of the best methods to deter criminals and give one peace of mind.

Statistical evidence seems to show that crime seems to be more of a fear than an actual problem. Yet there are some so-called street crimes that seem to affect more older adults. In particular, some of these crimes are: purse snatching, robbery, and hold-up. Bunco games, medical quacks, and fraudulent sales schemes have bilked untold numbers of people.

One thing that could be done as a part of this class is to organize an inspection tour of a home to check for security weakness. A security checklist could also be developed to distribute to the participants as well as a handout on crime-prevention hints. Contact individuals and agencies in your community which relate to crime involving the elderly.

Resource

National Criminal Justice System, Box 6000, Rockville, MD 20850

Elderhostel

The Elderhostel program began in 1975 for persons over sixty years of age to spend a few days to a week on a college campus. The senior adults live in the college dormitory and take several courses of interest offered through the program. In addition to the classroom educational program, the college may provide some sight-seeing opportunities in the area for those enrolled.

The cost for the week is nominal and normally includes room, board, and travel to and from the school. In most cases, the tuition is waived.

A church senior adult group could plan and promote a particular week for a summer educational opportunity trip. Upon returning, a mini "Elderhostel in Review" could be conducted at the church for those senior adults who were not able to attend. Those who participated in the Elderhostel could be the teachers of the event.

Resource

Elderhostel, 100 Boylston Street, Boston, MA 02116.

Trip and Travel

One of the fastest growing industries in our society is the travel industry. A majority of these persons are retirees. Travel meets a recreational social need for senior adults. It is one of the most popular components of most senior adult programs.

"Failing to Plan Is Planning to Fail"

Planning and coordination is essential if a travel ministry is to be effective. A Trip and Travel Committee needs to be elected from your senior adult group. A chairman or tour escort needs to be chosen to lead the committee in planning a balanced ministry. It is essential to plan around the interests of the group; therefore, a survey may need to be conducted. A balanced approach would be an annual extended tour, state and national events, and one-day trips. Keep in mind the financial needs of your people and the activity range of your seniors from very active to the frail elderly. Plan something for all.

One of the first tasks of the committee would be to develop trip and travel policies to govern your program. Below is a *sample* policy which speaks to the need.

Policy: Trip and Travel Committee

This component ministry (trip and travel) of the senior adult program is designed to provide socialization, education, and spiritual enrichment for the older adults of Calvary Baptist Temple. Those persons who are over age sixty and a Calvary Baptist will have first choice in reserving space on all trips. At a specified cutoff date, any person interested in reserving space will be welcomed.

Calvary Baptist Temple is self-supporting. Those persons participating in the trips pay their own expenses. No organization or any person receives profit from the tours. All trips are planned at cost; no profit is intended. The tour escort will be responsible for the details of promoting, planning, and coordinating all travel as chairperson of the Trip and Travel Committee. The committee plans a yearly schedule of trips with designated responsibilities to assist the tour escort. The tour escort is directly responsible to the minister of family enrichment.

The cost of each trip is determined by an estimate of exact need. The cost is established by the minister of family enrichment.

Refund Policy

Refunds are made only for cancellation due to illness, death, and the like. These refunds are awarded within the following procedures:
1. Prior to 45 days before a trip, all of the fee is refunded.
2. After 45 days before a trip, deposit is forfeited, and balance of money will be refunded.
3. When a replacement is provided by the person who cancels, all of the fee will be refunded.
4. Exceptions to the above policies may be made in hardship cases at the discretion of the minister of family enrichment.

Trip Insurance

Accident insurance has been added to all out-of-town packages. Coverage assures 24-hours-a-day protection. The insurance will be effective the moment the group leaves on their trip and continues throughout its duration.

PLEASE READ THE ABOVE CAREFULLY. ENROLLMENT IN AND PAYMENT FOR THE TRIP CONSTITUTES ACCEPTANCE OF THESE TRIP CONDITIONS.

---

10 Questions to Consider Before Travel

1. Where do we want to go?
2. How long will the trip be?
3. What is there to see and do along the route?
4. What type of transportation are we going to use?
5. Where and when will we eat?
6. Where will we spend the night?
7. How much is the total cost?
8. Have we made adequate plans for emergency medical/health needs?
9. Do we have a comfortable schedule of activities for the day?
10. Have we left adequate information for families and the church in case they need to contact us?

Emergencies

Hopefully none will occur, but if an emergency arises, will we be prepared? It is necessary to have some basic medical information on each person before the trip. Keep the information in a file with the tour escort. Below is a sample information form that could be used.

Senior Adult Emergency Information

Name_____   Telephone _____
Address_____   Birthdate_____
City_____   State_____Zip_____
Person to Notify in Case of Emergency:
Name_____   Relationship _____
Address_____   Telephone _____
City_____   State_____ Zip _____
Medicare Number: _____
What Medications Are You Allergic to? _____
What Medications Are You Currently Taking? ____
What Special Physical Condition Do You Have Which the Tour Leader Needs to Know? _____
In Case of Emergency, I Authorize the Above Information to Be Shared with the Medical Care Provider.

Signed _____

Date _____

Resource

See local travel agent for general information on planning travel opportunities.

7
Supplemental Information

Aging Demographics

Some facts gleaned from *Chartbook on Aging in America,* produced in preparation for the 1981 White House Conference on Aging; *A Profile of Older Americans* (a brochure); and *Aging America: Trends and Projections* (second printing, 1984), produced by American Association of Retired Persons:

Every twenty seconds, someone has a sixty-fifth birthday. Every day 3,800 Americans become sixty-five. Every day 3,000 Americans sixty-five or over die. Every day the group sixty-five and over increases by 800.

Persons sixty-five and older numbered 25.5 million according to the 1980 census. This represents 11.3 percent of the American population. The number of older Americans increased 28 percent from 1970 to 1980.

Presently one out of nine persons is sixty-five or older. By the year 2000, this will increase to one out of eight (13.1 percent) and this percentage may climb to one out of five (21.1 percent) by the year 2030. The most rapid increase for the over sixty-five group is expected to be from 2010 to 2030.

The older population is also aging. The 75-plus segment is the fastest growing age group in the US. In 1980, over 9 percent of the total 65-plus population was 85 or older. By the year 2010 this percentage will grow to 13 percent or more than 4.25 million. In 1980 there were more than 14,000 Americans one hundred years of age or older.

Life expectancy at birth reached a record 73.6 years in 1980, about twenty-six years longer than a child born in 1900. Persons reaching age sixty-five had an average expectancy of an additional 16.4 years (females to 83.4 and males to 79.1).

Children under eighteen years of age currently outnumber older Americans by 24 million, but both age groups will be equal in number shortly after the year 2015.

By 2025 older Americans will represent one third of the voting population of the United States compared to about one fifth today.

Would you believe there are more older women than men? In the age bracket 55-64, there are 112 women per 100 men. In the category 65-74 years of age, there are 131, and in the 75-84 age span, 166. In the 85-up age group, there are 229 women to 100 men.

More than half of all persons aged sixty-five and older are married and live in two-person, husband-and-wife households. Most older men are married (78 percent; 40 percent women) while most older women are widows. Seven out of ten women aged seventy-five and older are widows.

The majority of older persons live with a spouse or a relative in a family setting in a community. Only 5 percent of the over sixty-five age population live in institutions, but the percentage increases dramatically with age (1 percent for persons 65-74; 22 percent for persons 85 and over).

The proportion of men in the age group 55-65 who remain in the labor force is declining and has been for several years. In 1980, only one of five men age sixty-five or older was in the labor force. One third of all Social Security beneficiaries currently retire at age sixty-two. Older persons constitute 3 percent of the labor force (13 percent of older Americans were in the work force in 1980).

World population over sixty: According to the Population Reference Bureau, 8.7 percent of the 4.7 billion people who inhabit the planet are over sixty. The Bureau notes that life expectancy ranges from seventy-seven years in Iceland to forty in some African nations.

The educational level of the older population has been steadily increasing. In 1980, the elderly had completed an average of 10.2 years of education. About 41 percent had finished high school, and 9 percent had four or more years beyond high school.

Heart disease, cancer, and stroke accounted for over three fourths of all deaths in the sixty-five and older population. Heart disease alone accounts for nearly 45 percent of the deaths in this age group.

Old people have more chronic ailments than

young people. In most cases, these ailments aren't terribly limiting. But the likelihood of developing an ailment of a chronic nature increases dramatically with increasing age. Over 80 percent of older persons have at least one chronic condition, and multiple conditions are common. The most frequent are arthritis, hypertension, hearing impairment, heart conditions, visual impairment, and diabetes.

More than 1.3 million persons resided in nursing homes in 1977. Of these, 86 percent or 1.1 million were age sixty-five or older. This figure represents less than 5 percent of the total US population aged sixty-five or older. It is true, however, that the likelihood of spending part of one's life in a nursing home increases with age.

Only 5 percent of persons aged sixty-five or older suffer from severe senile dementia. The word *senile* has a long history of medical abuse. There are degenerative diseases of the brain which afflict older people. But senility is not, by any means, an inevitable consequence of growing old. And not every mental disorder in older people is the result of brain damage. What is diagnosed as "senility" may actually be the by-product of anemia, malnutrition, or infection. Such conditions may be fully reversible.

Persons 65 and older represent nearly one fourth of the membership of churches and synagogues in America. Religious organizations constitute by far the largest single network of voluntary community organizations serving the needs of the elderly in American society.

In 1978, persons sixty-five and older represented 11 percent of the US population but accounted for 29 percent of the total personal health care expenditures.

Older persons hold a major share of the nation's discretionary incomes, which is that money available to be spent on "nonessential" items.

Sample File System: Aging Topics (Reference)

AARP

Age Discrimination

Annuity Board

Attitudes

Aging (Biological)

Baptist Sunday School
    Board

Behavior

Bibliography

Bill of Rights

Blacks

Cancer

Career Pamphlets

Cartoons

Christian Life Commission

Church Activities

Community Centers

Community Programs

Conferences

Consumer Affairs

Continuing Education

Counseling

Crime and the Elderly

Culture

Day-care Center

Death and Dying

Depression

Disengagement Theory

Drug Abuse

Education

Employment

Evironment and the
    Elderly

Ethics

Euthanasia

Exercise Programs

Family Relationships

Federal Aid

Films
Food
Foreign Mission Board
Foster Grandparent
  Program
Foster Homes for the Aged
Frail Elderly
Geriatrics
Gerontological Society
Gerontology Training
Glossary
Governor's Committee on
  Aging
Grandparents
Gray Panthers
Handicapped
Health
Health Institutions
Health System Agencies
Home Mission Board
Home for the Aged
Hospice
Housing Authority
Humor
Insurance
Intelligence
Labor
Laws
Legislation
Leisure

Libraries
Longevity
Magazine Information
Mandatory Retirement
Marriage (Counseling)
Meals on Wheels
Medicaid
Medicare
Medical Problems
Medicine
Memory
Menopause
Mental Health
Mexican Americans
Milieu Therapy
Minorities
Music
Nutrition
Obesity
Older Americans Act
Older Women
Parents
Peace Corps
Pensions
Physical Fitness
Poems
Poverty
Preretirement Planning
Psychology
Public Health

Public Relations
Public Welfare
Recreation
Rehabilitation
Religion
Religious Material for the
    Elderly
Research
Retirement
Rural Elderly
Supplemental Security
Income (SSI)
Safety
Senior Centers
Sensory Loss
Sermons
Sex and Marriage
Social Problems
Social Security
Songs
Southern Baptist Associa-
    tion of Ministries with
    the Aging (SBAMA)

Speeches
Statistics
Stress
Stroke
Suicide
Taxes
Teenagers
Telephone Reassurance
Television
Therapy
Training, Sensitivity
Transportation
Travel and Vacations
Unemployment
Visual Disorders
Volunteers
White House Conference
    on Aging
Widows
Women
Youth and the Aged

8
Resources

Membership Organizations

Administration on Aging, U.S. Department of Health, Education and Welfare, 330 Independence Avenue, SW, Washington, DC 20221

American Association of Retired Persons (AARP), 1909 K Street, NW, Washington, DC 20048 (ask about *Action for Independent Maturity* also)

National Interfaith Coalition on Aging, 298 South Hull Street, Athens, GA 30605

Public Affairs Pamphlet, 381 Park Avenue, South, New York, NY 10016

Southern Baptist Association of Ministries with the Aging, 1350 Spring Street, NW, Atlanta, GA 30367-5601

The National Council on the Aging, Inc., 600 Maryland Avenue, SW, Washington, DC 20024

The Gerontological Society, 1835 K Street, NW, Suite 305, Washington, DC 20006

Western Gerontological Society, 785 Market Street, Suite 1114, San Francisco, CA 94103

Summer Workshops in Aging

Andrus Gerontology Center, University of Southern California, University Park, Los Angeles, CA 90007

The Institute of Gerontology, University of Michigan, 520 East Liberty Street, Ann Arbor, MI 48109

Center for Studies in Aging, North Texas State University, P. O. Box 13438, N.T. Stadium, Denton, TX 76203

Gerontological Program, Baylor University, Waco, TX 76798

Professional Periodicals

Aging, Superintendent of Documents, U. S. Government Printing Office, Washington, DC 20242

Aging and Work: a Journal on Age, Work and Retirement, National Council on the Aging, 18281 L Street, NW, Washington, DC 20036

Black Aging, National Council on Black Aging, Box 8522, Durham, NC 27707

Gerontologist, Gerontological Society, 1 Dupont Circle, Washington, DC 20035

Journal of Aging and Religion, Hayworth Press, 28 East 26th Street, New York, NY 10010

Journal of Geriatric Psychiatry, Boston Society of Gerontologic Psychiatry, 239 Park Avenue South, New York, NY

Journal of Gerontology, Gerontological Society, 1
   Dupont Circle, Washington, DC 20036

Social Security Bulletin, Superintendent of Documents, U. S. Government Printing Office, Washington, DC 20402

**Southern Baptist Convention Agencies and Boards
and Senior Adults**

Annuity Board, 511 North Akard Building, Dallas,
   Texas 75201; 214/720-0511.

Offers retirement program for church and
denominational employees and ministers.

Ministers to annuitants who receive monthly
checks.

1.   Leads Annuitants Conference at Ridgecrest
      Baptist Conference Center each year.
2.   Maintains a file of names of annuitants available
      for special service.
3.   Hosts annual annuitants breakfast during
      Southern Baptist Convention meeting.
4.   Conducts two annuitants' tours each year.
5.   Publishes monthly news sheets for the annuitants.
6.   Engages in a prayer ministry for annuitants.
7.   Ministers through field representatives across
      the Southern Baptist Convention.
8.   Provides relief ministry for annuitants who
      have dire needs. (Relief is also available to min-

isters or ministers' widows who never entered the retirement program.)

9.   Provides a retirement guidance program.

Baptist Sunday School Board, 127 Ninth Avenue, North Nashville, TN 37234; 615/251-2000.

Offers extensive programming and resources through the Family Ministry Department, Sunday School Department, and the Church Training Department.

Baptist Joint Committee on Public Affairs, 200 Maryland Avenue, NE, Washington, DC 20002; 202/544-4226.

This committee maintains vertical files on legislation on health and nutrition of aging and material on other aging legislation. Extensive files are maintained on housing for the elderly. Other reports maintained are of congressional hearings and legislation on aging.

Brotherhood Commission, 1548 Poplar Avenue, Memphis, TN 38104; 901/272-2461.

The Brotherhood Commission develops concepts, services, and materials for men, including the aging, which focus on missions. They also sponsor short-term projects or mission tours which involve older persons on a volunteer basis.

Christian Life Commission, 901 Commerce Street, Nashville, TN 37203; 615/244-2495. Executive Director: Larry Baker.

The Christian Life Commission emphasizes the need for concern about issues which affect senior adults. The staff speaks, writes, and works in support of increased awareness of the aging and their needs. They also distribute literature on aging.

Foreign Mission Board, P. O. Box 6597, Richmond, VA 23230; 804/353-0151. Executive Director: R. Keith Parks.

The Foreign Mission Board ministers to the aging in missionary work around the world dealing with needs relating to aging among missionaries themselves. The Board sponsors volunteer projects through which older adults may serve in extended service, short-term service, and the Mission Service Corps.

Historical Commission, 901 Commerce Street, Nashville, TN 37203; 615/244-0344. Executive Director: Lynn E. May, Jr.

The Historical Commission publishes a quarterly journal: *Baptist History and Heritage,* channeling articles on Baptist heritage through state Baptist newspapers and other Baptist periodicals. They utilize "oral history" as a means of gathering information from those who have helped to make Southern Baptist history.

Home Mission Board, 1350 Spring Street, NW, Atlanta, GA 30309; 404/873-4041. Executive Director-Treasurer: Larry L. Lewis.

The Home Mission Board provides a program of preretirement planning for personnel. They give support and encouragement to retired missionaries with membership in AARP and paid visits to one of the summer assemblies about every third year. They provide programs for the aging through the Christian Social Ministries Department and sponsor volunteer projects through which older adults may serve.

Southern Baptist Foundation, 901 Commerce Street, Nashville, TN 37203; 615/254-8823.

The Foundation provides financial services whereby older persons can make investments in Southern Baptist work.

Woman's Missionary Union, Highway 280, East, 100 Missionary Ridge, Birmingham, AL 35243-2798; 205/991-8100. Executive Director: Carolyn Weatherford.

The WMU promotes the organization of mission action groups to minister to the aging. They encourage older persons to participate in volunteer mission service programs through the Home Mission and Foreign Mission Boards. The WMU participates in the Senior Adult Chautauqua sponsored by the Sunday School Board.

Southern Baptist Association of Ministries
With the Aging

The Southern Baptist Association of Ministries with the Aging(SBAMA) began as the Southern Baptist Executives of Homes for the Aging in 1963. In 1977 it was expanded to include people involved at all levels of Southern Baptist work with the aging.

Purpose

The purpose of this association shall be to bring together persons vocationally involved in ministry with the aging in order to:

1. Promote quality care for the residents in Baptist homes for the aging.
2. Foster the development of church and denominational ministries to help meet the needs of the aging in our society.
3. Encourage the development of curriculum and professional training programs in Southern Baptist higher education.
4. Advocate continuing research in the field of aging.
5. Cooperate in sharing information and planning programs that shall be beneficial to all members concerned.
6. Encourage recruitment and placement of people in vocations with the aging.
7. Enhance awareness of need for and potential in meeting needs of older persons.

State Convention Senior Adult Programs

Alabama: Box 11870, Montgomery AL 36111; 205/ 288-2460

Alaska: Star Route A, Box 1791, Anchorage, AK 99507; 907/344-9627

Arizona: 400 West Camelback Road, Phoenix, AZ 85013; 602/264-9421

Arkansas: Box 552, Little Rock, AR 72203; 501/ 376-4791

California: Box 1568, 678 East Shaw, Fresno, CA 9355; 209/229-9533

Colorado: 7393 South Alton Way, Englewood, CO 80112; 303/771-2480

District of Columbia: 1628 Sixteenth Street, NW, Washington, DC 20009; 202/265-1526

Florida: 1230 Hendricks Avenue, Jacksonville, FL 32207; 904/396-2351

Georgia: 2930 Flowers Road, South, Atlanta, GA 30341; 404/455-0404

Hawaii: 2042 Vancouver, Honolulu, HI 96822; 808/946-9581

Illinois: Box 3486, Springfield, IL 62708; 217/786-2600

Indiana: Box 24038, Indianapolis, IN 46224; 317/ 241-9317

Iowa: Westview, #27, 2400 86th Street, Des Moines, IA 50322; 515/274-2420

Kansas-Nebraska: 5410 West 7th, Topeka, KS 66606; 913/273-4880

Kentucky: Box 43433, Middletown, KY 40243; 502/245-4101

Louisiana: Box 311, Alexandria, LA 71301; 318/448-3402, ext. 232

Maryland: 1313 York Road, Lutherville, MD 21093; 301/321-7900

Michigan: 15635 West 12 Mile Road, Southfield, MI 48076; 313/557-4200

Minnesota-Wisconsin: 519 16th Street, SE, Rochester, MN 55904-5296; 507/282-3636

Mississippi: Box 530, Jackson, MS 39205; 601/968-3800

Missouri: 400 East High Street, Jefferson City, MO 65101; 314/635-7931

Nevada: 895 North Center Street, Reno, NV 89501; 702/322-0895

New England: P.O. Box 313, Northboro, MA 01532; 617/393-6013

New Mexico: P.O. Box 485, Albuquerque, NM 87103; 505/247-0586

New York: 500 South Salina Street, Syracuse, NY 13202; 315/475-6173

North Carolina: P.O. Box 26508, Raleigh, NC 27611; 919/467-5100

Northern Plains: P.O. Box 1278, Rapid City, SD 57709; 605/343-5572

Northwest: 1033 Northeast 6th, Portland, OR 97232; 503/238-4545

Ohio: 1680 East Broad, Columbus, OH 43203

Oklahoma: 1141 North Robinson, Oklahoma City, OK 73103; 405/236-4341

Pennsylvania-South New Jersey: 620 Fritchey Street, Harrisburg, PA 17109; 717/652-8556

South Carolina: 907 Richland Street, Columbia, SC 29201; 803/765-0030

Tennessee: P.O. Box 728, Brentwood, TN 37027; 615/373-2255

Texas: 703 North Ervay Street, Dallas, TX 75201; 214/741-1991

Utah-Idaho: Box 1039, Sandy, UT 84092; 801/322-3565

Virginia: P.O. Box 8568, Richmond, VA 23226; 804/282-9751

West Virginia: 801 Sixth Avenue, Saint Albans, WV 25177; 304/727-2974

Wyoming: P.O. Box 3074, Casper, WY 82601; 307/577-1451

State Agencies Concerned with Aging

Alabama: Commission of Aging, 740 Madison Avenue, Montgomery, AL 36104.

Alaska: Office on Aging, Department of Health and Social Services, Pouch H, Juneau, AK 99801.

Arizona: Bureau on Aging, Department of Economic Security, 543 East McDowell Road, Phoenix, AZ 85004.

Arkansas: Department on Aging, Department of Social and Rehabilitation Service, 4313 West

Markham, Hendrix Hall, P.O. Box 2179, Little Rock, AR 72203.

California: Office on Aging, Health and Welfare Agency, 455 Capitol Mall, Suite 500, Sacramento, CA 95814.

Colorado: Division of Services for the Aging, Department of Social Services, 1575 Sherman Street, Denver, CO 80203.

Connecticut: Department on Aging, 90 Washington Street, Room 312, Hartford, CT 06115.

Delaware: Division of Aging, Department of Health and Social Services, 2407 Lancaster Avenue, Wilmington, DE 19805.

District of Columbia: Division of Services to the Aged, Department of Human Resources, 1329 East Street, NW, Washington, DC 20004.

Florida: Division of Aging, Department of Health and Rehabilitation Service, 1317 Winewood Boulevard, Building 3, Fourth Floor, Tallahassee, FL 32301.

Georgia: Office of Aging, Department of Human Resources, 618 Ponce de Leon Avenue, Atlanta, GA 30308.

Guam: Office of Aging, Social Service Administration, Government of Guam, Box 2816, Agana, Guam 96910.

Hawaii: Commission on Aging, 1149 Bethel Street, Room 311, Honolulu, HI 96813.

Idaho: Office on Aging, Department of Special Service, Capital Annex #7, 509 North 5th Street, Boise, ID 83720.

Illinois: Department on Aging, 2401 West Jefferson, Springfield, IL 62706.

Indiana: Commission on Aging and the Aged, Graphic Arts Building, 215 North Senate Avenue, Indianapolis, IN 46202.

Iowa: Commission on Aging, 415 West 10th Street, Jewett Building, Des Moines, IA 50319.

Kansas: Division of Social Service, Services for the Aging Section, Department of Social and Rehabilitation Service, State Office Building, Topeka, KA 66612.

Kentucky: Aging Program Unit, Department of Human Resources, 413 Wapping Street, Frankfort, KY 40601.

Louisiana: Bureau of Aging, Division of Human Resources, Health and Social and Rehabilitation Service Administration, Box 44282, Capitol Station, Baton Rouge, LA 70804.

Maine: Office of Maine's Elderly, Community Service Unit, Department of Health and Welfare, State House, Augusta, ME 04330.

Maryland: Commission on Aging, State Office Building, 1123 North Eui, Baltimore, MD 21201.

Massachusetts: Executive Office of Affairs, State

Office Building, 18 Tremont Street, Boston, MA 02109.

Michigan: Office of Service to the Aging, 1026 East Michigan Avenue, Lansing, MI 48912.

Minnesota: Governor's Citizen's Council on Aging, 690 North Robert Street, Saint Paul, MN 55155.

Mississippi: Council on Aging, Foundren Station, 2906 North State Street, Jackson, MS 39216.

Missouri: Office of Aging, Division of Special Services, Department of Social Services, Broadway State Office Building, Box 570, Jefferson City, MO 65101.

Montana: Aging Service Bureau, Department of Social and Rehabilitation Service, Box 1723, Helena, MT 59601.

Nebraska: Commission on Aging, State House Station 94784, 300 South 17th Street, Lincoln, NE 68509.

Nevada: Division of Aging, Department of Human Resources, 201 South Fall Street, Room 300, Nye Building, Carson City, NV 89701.

New Hampshire: Council on Aging, Box 786, 14 Depot Street, Concord, NH 03301.

New Jersey: Office on Aging, Department of Community Affairs, Box 2768, 363 West State Street, Trenton, NJ 08625.

New Mexico: Commission on Aging, 408 Gallsteo-Villagra Building, Santa Fe, NM 87501.

New York: Office for the Aging, New York State Executive Department, 855 Central Avenue, Albany, NY 12206.

North Carolina: Governor's Coordinating Council on Aging, Department of Human Resources, Administration Building, 213 Hillsborough Street, Raleigh, NC 27603.

North Dakota: Aging Services, Department of Social Services, State Capitol Building, Bismarck, ND 58501.

Ohio: Commission on Aging, 34 North High Street, Columbus, OH 43215.

Oklahoma: Special Unit on Aging, Department of Institutions, Social Rehabilitative Services, Box 25352, Capitol Station, Oklahoma, OK 73125.

Oregon: Program on Aging, Human Resources Department, 315 Public Service Building, Salem, OR 97310.

Pennsylvania: Office for the Aging, Department of Public Welfare, Capital Associated Building, Harrisburg, PA 17120.

Puerto Rico: Gericulture Commission, Department of Social Services, Apartado 11697, Santurce, PR 00910.

Rhode Island: Division on Aging, Department of Community Affairs, 150 Washington Street, Providence, RI 02903.

Samoa: Government of American Samos, Office of

the Governor, Pago Pago, American Samoa 96920.

South Carolina: Program on Aging, 915 Main Street, Columbia, SC 29201.

South Dakota: Program on Aging, Department of Social Services, Saint Charles Hotel, Pierre, SD 57501.

Tennessee: Commission on Aging, 706 Church Street, Suite 201, Nashville, TN 37219.

Texas: Governor's Committee on Aging, Box 12786, Capitol Station, Austin, TX 78711.

Trust Territory of the Pacific: Office of the Aging, Community Development Division, Governor of the Trust Territory of the Pacific Islands, Saipan, Mariana Islands 96950.

Utah: Division of Aging, Department of Social Services, 345 South 6th Street, Salt Lake City, UT 84102.

Vermont: Office on Aging, Department of Human Services, 56 State Street, Montpelier, VT 05602.

Virginia: Office on Aging, Division of State Planning and Community Affairs, 9 North 12th Street, Richmond, VA 23219.

Washington: Office on Aging, Department of Social & Health Services, Box 1788-M.S., 45-2, 410 West Fifth, Olympia, WA 98504.

West Virginia: Commission on Aging, State Capitol, Charleston, WV 25305.

Wisconsin: Division on Aging, Department of Health & Social Services, 1 West Wilson Street, Room 686, Madison, WI 53702.

Wyoming: Aging Services, Department of Health & Social Services, Division of Public Assistance & Social Services, State Office Building, Cheyenne, WY 82002.

National Resource List

American Aging Association, University of Nebraska Medical Center, Omaha, NE 68105.

American Association of Homes for the Aging, 1050 17th Street, NW, Washington, DC 20036.

American Association of Retired Persons, 215 Long Beach Boulevard, Long Beach, CA 90801.

American Cancer Society, 219 East 42nd Street, New York, NY 10021.

American Diabetes Association, 18 East 48th Street, New York, NY 10017.

American Foundation for the Blind, Inc., 15 West 16th Street, New York, NY 10011.

American Geriatrics Society, 10 Columbus Circle, New York, NY 10011.

American Health Care Association, 2500 15th Street, NW, Washington, DC 20006.

American Heart Association, 44 West 23rd Street, New York, NY 10010.

American Lung Association, 1740 Broadway, New York, NY 10019.

American Physical Therapy Association, 1740 Broadway, New York, NY 10019.

American Red Cross, 17th and D Streets, NW, Washington, DC 20006.

Andrus Gerontology Center, University of Southern California, Los Angeles, CA 90007.

Association of Rehabilitation Facilities, 5530 Wisconsin Avenue, NW, Washington, DC 20015.

Center for the Study of Aging and Human Development, Duke University, Durham, NC 27710.

Concern for Dying (an educational council), 250 West 57th Street, New York, NY 10107.

Continental Association for Funeral and Memorial Societies, 1828 L Street, NW, Washington, DC 20036.

Elderhostel, 100 Boylston Street, Suite 200, Boston, MA 02116.

Episcopal Society for Ministry on Aging, Inc., RFD #1, Box 28, Milford, NJ 08848.

Family Service Association of America, 44 West 23rd Street, New York, NY 10010.

Gerontological Society, 1 Dupont Circle, Washington, DC 20036.

Gray Panthers, 3635 Chestnut Street, Philadelphia, PA 19104.

Hogg Foundation for Mental Health, The University of Texas, Austin, TX 78712.

Homemakers' Home and Health Care Services, 3651 Van Rick Drive, Kalamazoo, MI 49001.

Jewish Guild for the Blind, 15 West 65th Street, New York, NY 10023.

National Association for Mental Health, 1800 North Kent Street, Arlington, VA 22209.

National Association for the Deaf, 814 Thayer Avenue, Silver Springs, MD 20910.

National Association of Hearing and Speech Agencies, 814 Thayer Avenue, Silver Spring, MD 20910.

National Caucus on the Black Aged, 1730 M Street, NW, Washington, DC 20036.

National Council on the Aging, Suite 504, 1828 L Street, NW, Washington, DC 20036.

National Council for Homemaker-Home Health Aide Service, 67 Irving Place, New York, NY 10003.

National Council of Senior Citizens, 1511 K Street, NW, Room 202, Washington, DC 20005.

National Interfaith Coalition on Aging, Inc., P.O. Box 1986, Indianapolis, IN 46206.

National Retired Teachers Association, 1901 K Street, NW, Washington, DC 20036.

New Eyes for the Needy, Inc., Short Hills, NJ 07078.

Pacific Garden Mission, 646 South State Street, Chicago, IL 60605.

Preventicare, Lawrence Frankle Foundation, Virginia and Brooks Street, Charleston, WV 25301.

Reigner Recording Library, Union Theological Seminary, Richmond VA 23227.

Southern Baptist Association of Ministries with the Aging, Home Mission Board, 1350 Spring Street, NW, Atlanta, GA 30367-5601.

U. S. Administration on Aging, 3303 C Street, SW, HHS South, Washington, DC 20024.

9
Bibliography

Bibliography

Activities and Programming

Burger, Isabel B. *Creative Drama for Senior Adults.* Morehouse: Barlow Company, 1980.

Carlson, Adelle. *Four Seasons Party and Banquet Book.** Nashville: Broadman Press, 1965.

Howell, Sarah. *Creative Crafts for Self-Expression.** Nashville: Broadman Press, 1978.

Miller, Sarah Walton. *Drama for Senior Adults.* Nashville: Broadman Press, 1978.

Sessoms, Bob. *150 Ideas for Activities with Senior Adults.* Nashville: Broadman Press, 1977.

Sessoms, Bob and Carolyn. *52 Complete Recreation Programs for Senior Adults.* Nashville: Convention Press, 1979.

Vickery, Florence. *Creative Programming for Senior Adults.* New York: Association Press, 1972.

Administration

Kader, Raymond A. *Senior Adult Utilization and Ministry Handbook.* Nashville: Broadman Press, 1976.

*Out of print. Check with your church library.

147

Kerr, Horace L. *How to Minister to Senior Adults in Your Church.* Nashville: Broadman Press, 1980.

Gray, Robert M., and Moberg, David O. *The Church and the Older Person.* Grand Rapids: Eerdmans Publishing Co., 1977.

Prevost, Tom E. *Aging—Senior Impact: Handbook on Aging and Senior Adult Ministries.* Atlanta: Home Mission Board, 1976.

Gerontological Studies

Atchley, Robert C. *The Social Forces in Later Life: An Introduction to Social Gerontology.* Belmont, Calif.: Wadsworth Publishers, 1972.

Freeman, Carroll B. *The Senior Adult Years: A Christian Psychology of Aging.* Nashville: Broadman Press, 1979.

Schwartz, Arthur N. and Peterson, James A. *Introduction to Gerontology.* New York: Holt, Rinehart, and Winston, 1979.

Silverstone, Barbara and Hyman, Helen Kandel. *You and Your Aging Parents: The Modern Family's Guide to Emotional, Physical, and Financial Problems.* New York: Pantheon Books, 1977.

Cassette Tapes

Dye, Harold. *The Touch of Friendship.* Nashville: Broadman, 1980.

Mead, J. Earl. *Meditations from the Mountains.** Nashville: Broadman, 1978.

Pylant, Agnes. *God Talks with a Senior Adult,* adapted by permission (Broadman) from *If God Talked Out Loud* by Clyde Lee Herring. Nashville: Broadman, 1978.

The Best of Agnes Pylant. Nashville: Broadman, 1979.

Steen, John Warren. *Themes for Mature Living.** Nashville: Broadman, 1979.

* Out of print. Check with your church library.

Catalogs
Gerontological Film Collection. Center for Studies in Aging, North Texas State University, Box 13438, NT Station, Denton, Texas 76203.

Films and Filmstrips
Volunteer to Live. The Communications Commission Film Rental.

Harris, Louis Associates. *The Myth and Reality of Aging in America.* National Council on the Aging, Inc.

Senior Adult Musicals
Backes, Greg. *Age Isn't Really Important.* Harrisburg: Backes Music, 1983.

Bartlett, Gene, Hawthorne, Grace and Brown,

Charles F. *Shadetree Musician.* Waco, Texas: Word Music, 1983.

Huff, R. G., Sloan, Bill, and Braman, Barry. *More Than Ever Before.* Nashville: Broadman Press, 1984.

Miller, Sarah Walton and Madaris, Don. *Count on Us.* Nashville: Light Hearted Music Publishing Co., 1977.

Oldenburg, Bob and Allen, Lanny. *Kingdom Within.* Nashville: Broadman Press, 1981.

Parks, Joe. *The Time of Our Lives.* Singspiration, 1984.

Robinson, Robert B. *He's My Father.* Marshall: Robin Song, 1984.

Robinson, B. *All My Life.* Marshall: Robin Song, 1983.

Robinson, Robert B. *It's a Beautiful Day.* Marshall: Robin Song, 1984.

Woolley, Bob, and Kirkland, Terry. *Saints Alive.* Nashville, Triune, 1982.

Woolley, Bob, and Kirkland, Terry. *Saints Alive in Prime Time.* Nashville, Triune, 1984.

Woolley, Bob, and Kirkland, Terry. *Saints Alive on Tour.* Nashville, Triune, 1 May 1985.

Retirement Planning

Uris, Auren. *Over 50—the Definitive Guide to Retire-*

ment. Philadelphia: Chilton Book Company, 1979.

Collins, Thomas. *The Complete Guide to Retirement.* New York: Prentice-Hall, Inc., 1977.

Videotapes

Conducting a Senior Adult Day. A 15-minute videotape presentation illustrating what one church did in conjunction with Senior Adult Day. Broadman Consumer Sales, Nashville, TN 37234.

Southern Baptist Response to the Needs of the Elderly by Horace Kerr, Broadman Consumer Sales, Nashville, TN 1983. (1/2 inch VHS, 15 minutes.)

About the Author

Roger L. Hauser is minister of family enrichment at Calvary Baptist Temple in Savannah, Georgia. He is responsible for coordinating single, young/median, senior adult, and age-integrated family ministries.

Hauser holds several honors and degrees, including a Master's degree in Religious Education from Southwestern Baptist Theological Seminary, Fort Worth, Texas. There he specialized in adult education. In addition, he has earned a Master of Science degree in Gerontology from North Texas State University.

Roger has had a varied background in senior adult work. He has served nursing homes as an activity and program director. While living in Texas, he was a senior adult intern with the Christian Life Commission of the Baptist General Convention of Texas and an organizer and president of the Southwestern Baptist Theological Seminary chapter of the Southern Baptist Association of Ministries with the Aging. Later he became the president of the Southern Baptist Association of Ministries with the Aging. Moving to Savannah to serve Calvary Baptist Temple as minister of senior adults, he was active with local boards in the community. From there he became senior adult leadership training consultant with the Senior Adult Section of the Family Ministry Department, Baptist Sunday School Board, Nashville, Tennessee. Roger then was called back to Savannah in an expanded church role at Calvary Baptist Temple.

Hauser has written chapters for two Convention Press books, *Achieving Wholeness in Later Life,* edited by Jack Gulledge, and *How God Called,* edited by Alice Magill (a testimony of his call to senior adult ministry). He has also written for several Southern Baptist periodicals and for *The Christian Index,* the Georgia Baptist paper (a series of twelve articles on aging).

Roger is married to Donna Lynn Williford of Savannah. Donna is a former licensed nursing home activity director and assists Roger in activity idea workshops. Roger and Donna have two children, Lauren and David.

HORACE L. KERR
Manager, Senior and Single Adult Section
Family Ministry Department
Baptist Sunday School Board